MW01235275

More than **200,000** student reviews on nearly **7,000** schools!

SEE IT ALL ON COLLEGEPROWLER.COM!

This book only offers a glimpse at our extensive coverage of one school out of thousands across the country. Visit *collegeprowler.com* to view our full library of content for FREE! Our site boasts thousands of photos and videos, interactive search tools, more reviews, and expanded content on nearly 7,000 schools.

CONNECT WITH SCHOOLS

Connect with the schools you are most interested in and discover new schools that match your interests.

FIND SCHOLARSHIPS

We give away $2,000 each month and offer personalized matches from a database of more than 3.2 million other scholarships!

SELECT A MAJOR

We have information on every major in the country to help you choose your degree and plan your career.

USE OUR TOOLS TO HELP YOU CHOOSE

Compare schools side-by-side, estimate your chances of admission, and get personalized school recommendations.

To get started, visit _collegeprowler.com/register_

Florida State University

Tallahassee, FL

Written by Cheryl Justis, Richard Bist

Edited by the College Prowler Team

ISBN # 978-1-4274-0425-1

©Copyright 2011 College Prowler

All Rights Reserved
Printed in the U.S.A.
www.collegeprowler.com

Last updated: 3/23/2011

College Prowler®
5001 Baum Blvd.
Suite 750
Pittsburgh, PA 15213

Phone: (800) 290-2682
Fax: (800) 772-4972
E-Mail: info@collegeprowler.com
Web: www.collegeprowler.com

How this all started...

When I was trying to find the perfect college, I used every resource that was available to me. I went online to visit school Web sites; I talked with my high school guidance counselor; I read book after book; I hired a private counselor. Sure, this was all very helpful, but nothing really told me what life was like at the schools I cared about. These sources weren't giving me enough information to be totally confident in my decision.

In all my research, there were only two ways to get the information I wanted.

The first was to physically visit the campuses and see if things were really how the brochures described them, but this was quite expensive and not always feasible. The second involved a missing ingredient: the students. Actually talking to a few students at those schools gave me a taste of the information that I needed so badly. The problem was that I wanted more but didn't have access to enough people.

In the end, I weighed my options and decided on a school that felt right and had a great academic reputation, but truth be told, the choice was still very much a crapshoot. I had done as much research as any other student, but was I 100 percent positive that I had picked the school of my dreams?

Absolutely not.

My dream in creating College Prowler was to build a resource that people can use with confidence. My own college search experience taught me the importance of gaining true insider insight; that's why the majority of this guide is composed of quotes from actual students. After all, shouldn't you hear about a school from the people who know it best?

I hope you enjoy reading this book as much as we've enjoyed putting it together. Tell me what you think when you get a chance. I'd love to hear your college selection stories.

Luke Skurman
CEO and Co-Founder
luke@collegeprowler.com

Welcome to College Prowler®

When we created College Prowler, we felt it was critical that our content was unbiased and unaffiliated with any college or university. We think it's important that our readers get honest information and a realistic impression of the student opinions on any campus—that's why if any aspect of a particular school is terrible, we (unlike a campus brochure) intend to publish it. While we do keep an eye out for the occasional extremist—the cheerleader or the cynic—we take pride in letting the students tell it like it is. We strive to create a book that's as representative as possible of each particular campus. Our books cover both the good and the bad, and whether the survey responses point to recurring trends or a variation in opinion, these sentiments are directly and proportionally expressed through our guides.

College Prowler guidebooks are in the hands of students throughout the entire process of their creation. Because you can't make student-written guides without the students, we have students at each campus who help write, randomly survey their peers, edit, layout, and perform accuracy checks on every book that we publish. From the very beginning, student writers gather the most up-to-date stats, facts, and inside information on their colleges. They fill each section with student quotes and summarize the findings in editorial reviews. In addition, each school receives a collection of letter grades (A through F) that reflect student opinion and help to represent contentment or satisfaction for each of our 20 specific categories. Just as in grade school, the higher the mark the more content or more satisfied the students are with the particular category.

Each book is the result of endless student contributions, hundreds of pages of research and writing, and countless hours of hard work. All of this has led to the creation of a student information network that stretches across the nation to every school that we cover. It's no easy accomplishment, but it's the reason that our guides are such a great resource.

When reading our books and looking at our grades, keep in mind that every college is different and that the students who make up each school are not uniform—as a result, it is important to assess schools on a case-by-case basis. Because it's impossible to summarize an entire school with a single number or description, each book provides a dialogue, not a decision, that's made up of 20 different topics and hundreds of student quotes. In the end, we hope that this guide will serve as a valuable tool in your college selection process. Enjoy!

The College Prowler Team

Table of Contents

By the Numbers

School Contact
Florida State University
211 Westcott Bldg
Tallahassee, FL 32306

Control:
Public

Academic Calendar:
Semester

Religious Affiliation:
None

Founded:
1851

Web Site:
www.fsu.edu

Main Phone:
(850) 644-2525

Student Body
Full-Time Undergraduates:
27,704

Part-Time Undergraduates:
3,099

Total Male Undergraduates:
14,918

Total Female Undergraduates:
18,287

Admissions
Acceptance Rate:
61%

Total Applicants:
23,439

Total Acceptances:
14,308

Freshman Enrollment:
5,967

Yield (% of admitted students who enroll):
42%

Applicants Placed on Waiting List:
1,907

Applicants Accepting a Place on Waiting List:
667

Students Enrolled from Waiting List:
277

Transfer Applications Received:
6,621

Transfer Applications Accepted:
3,118

Transfer Students Enrolled:
2,086

Transfer Application Acceptance Rate:
47%

SAT I or ACT Required?
Either

SAT I Range (25th–75th Percentile):
1110–1290

SAT I Verbal Range (25th–75th Percentile):
550–640

SAT I Math Range (25th–75th Percentile):
560–650

ACT Composite Range (25th–75th Percentile):
24–28

ACT English Range (25th–75th Percentile):
22–28

ACT Math Range (25th–75th Percentile):
22–26

Top 10% of High School Class:
31%

Application Fee:
$30

Common Application Accepted?
No

Admissions Phone:
(850) 644-6200

Admissions E-Mail:
admissions@admin.fsu.edu

Admissions Web Site:
admissions.fsu.edu/

Regular Decision Deadline:
January 21

Regular Decision Notification:
March 28

Must-Reply-By Date:
May 1

Financial Information

In-State Tuition:
$4,566

Out-of-State Tuition:
$19,011

Room and Board:
$8,000

Books and Supplies:
$1,000

Average Amount of Federal Grant Aid:
$3,726

Percentage of Students Who Received Federal Grant Aid:
16%

Average Amount of Institution Grant Aid:
$2,246

Percentage of Students Who Received Institution Grant Aid:
36%

Average Amount of State Grant Aid:
$3,140

Percentage of Students Who Received State Grant Aid:
91%

Average Amount of Student Loans:
$3,187

Percentage of Students Who Received Student Loans:
28%

Total Need-Based Package:
$4,107

Percentage of Students Who Received Any Aid:
96%

Financial Aid Forms Deadline:
Rolling

Financial Aid Phone:
(850) 644-0539

Financial Aid E-Mail:
ofacs@admin.fsu.edu

Financial Aid Web Site:
financialaid.fsu.edu/

Academics

The Lowdown On...
Academics

Degrees Awarded
Associate degree
Bachelor's degree
Master's degree
Post-master's certificate

Most Popular Majors
Criminal Justice and Safety Studies
English Language Studies
Finance, General
Psychology

Majors Offered
Architecture and Planning
Arts
Biological Sciences
Business
Communications
Computer and Sciences
Education
Engineering
Health Care
Languages and Literature
Law
Mathematics & Statistics
Philosophy and Religion
Physical Sciences

Protective Services
Psychology & Counseling
Recreation & Fitness
Social Sciences & Liberal Arts
Social Services

Undergraduate Schools/Divisions

College of Arts & Sciences
College of Business
College of Communication
College of Criminology and Criminal Justice
College of Education
College of Engineering
College of Human Sciences
College of Information
College of Motion Picture, Television, and Recording Arts
College of Music
College of Nursing
College of Social Sciences and Public Policy
College of Social Work
College of Visual Arts, Theatre, and Dance

Full-Time Instructional Faculty

1,312

Part-Time Instructional Faculty

329

Faculty with Terminal Degree

92%

Average Faculty Salary

$79,237

Student-Faculty Ratio

25:1

Class Sizes

Fewer than 20 Students: 34%
20 to 49 Students: 52%
50 or More Students: 14%

Full-Time Retention Rate

89%

Part-Time Retention Rate

71%

Graduation Rate

70%

Remedial Services?

No

Academic/Career Counseling?

Yes

Instructional Programs
Occupational: No
Academic: Yes
Continuing Professional: Yes
Recreational/Avocational: Yes
Adult Basic Remedial: No
Secondary (High School): No

Special Credit Opportunities
Advanced Placement (AP)
Credits: Yes
Dual Credit: Yes
Life Experience Credits: No

Special Study Options
Distance learning
opportunities
Study abroad
Teacher certification (below
the postsecondary level)

Best Places to Study

Dirac Library
Starbucks
Strozier Library

Did You Know?

Current faculty members include Pulitzer Prize winner Robert Olen Butler, as well as former astronauts, Dr. Norm Thagard and Captain Winston Scott, who teach in the College of Engineering.

The Carnegie Foundation has designated Florida State University as a Research 1 University for the Advancement of Teaching. FSU's Center for Advanced Power Systems was awarded a $52 million grant by the U.S. Navy for use in testing propulsion systems.

Students Speak Out On...
Academics

Q Music Therapy Changed My Life

The Music Therapy department at the College of Music at Florida State University is one of the top in the nation. The professors are some of the most knowledgeable and influential leaders in the field of Music Therapy. They are incredibly helpful and want to prepare their students the best they possibly can for real life experience. There are tons of internship possibilities that suit the student's individual needs and interests. The workload is reasonable, but is structured to push the students. I had no idea what Music Therapy was before I came to FSU, but this program has opened my eyes to a career perfectly suited for me.

Q Academic Process

Academics offered at my school are amazing. There is something for everyone and the school strives to cater to everyone's needs and interest. The registration process is easy and the advisors are readily available to help students when needed. Professors encourage students to ask for help and are very flexible when it comes to meeting with students to discuss the class and any problems they may have.

Q Communications Major

I'm a Communications Major and currently applying for the Communications College at Florida State. I have taken some communication classes. The staff are extremely interested in their work and are always there to help the students. The material learned intrigues me as well as challenges me to move forward in my studies as well as excel. I volunteer at the Florida State radio station, V89, by working with the Public Relations department. I attend different concerts and meet with band members to help promote the station. I'm also a member of FPRA (Florida Public Relations Association). I attend weekly meetings for both facilities as well as participate in seminars when offered.

Q Art History Department

The art history department is honestly fabulous. Classes are challenging, but professors are always willing to answer questions and love class participation. Internship opportunities are quite common and our advisers do their best to let everyone know as soon as they hear about a new opportunity.

Q A Great Education

As an Undergraduate, I have been in courses that everybody has to take. All of them have been great so far. Registration is easy, especially if you're in the honors program. Florida State offers plenty of fun, relevant courses and the professors here are nothing short of excellent. In my first year, I was already able to get recommendations.

Q Instrumental Music Education

Being a Music Education major is the joy of my life. It requires much work outside of the classroom, including concerts and teacher observations. Although it takes so much time, it is very rewarding. The professors are spectacular and have acquired so much experience they never run out of events to share and talk about. The classes may seem irrelevant at the time, but in the end they all strong together to one joint education. GO NOLES

Q Helpful for Freshmen

I'm a freshman with an intended major of criminology. The Criminology department has advised me on what to take to help achieve my goals, and they have been very helpful and welcoming in general.

ℚ Florida State

Overall, my experience at Florida State has been a good one. All of the professors are very easy to talk to willing to help (even in large lecture classes). There is a wide assortment of classes for those who wish to dabble in other subjects and plenty of interesting courses to complete your requirements.

The College Prowler Take On...
Academics

The consensus among the Florida State University student body is that the faculty is both easy to get along with and dedicated to its profession. Most instructors are readily available to meet with students outside of class and offer assistance when necessary. No professor wants to see a student fail, but don't expect them to cater to you. Take the initiative, and they'll respect you for it. A lot of the professors make themselves available to the students, either by providing contact information (such as phone numbers and e-mail addresses) or by holding office hours, in which the students can talk to their professors one-on-one. Most students admit that the prolific number of teaching assistants can be problematic in the lower-level classes. However, word of mouth is an excellent way to find out in advance which professors to take and which to avoid. That's what upperclassmen are there for!

Academics are important at Florida State University, especially among the tenured professors. Don't expect to coast through the higher-level undergraduate classes. It's college; you're here for the academics, so expect to work hard. The teaching assistants and associate professors are more likely to cut you some slack, but even that isn't a guarantee. The school has received recognition for a broad range of research projects, and they have just created a new College of Medicine.

B

The College Prowler® Grade on
Academics: B

A high Academics grade generally indicates that professors are knowledgeable, accessible, and genuinely interested in their students' welfare. Other determining factors include class size, how well professors communicate, and whether or not classes are engaging.

Local Atmosphere

The Lowdown On...
Local Atmosphere

City, State
Tallahassee, FL

Setting
Mid-sized city

Distances to Nearest Major Cities
Jacksonville – FL – 3 hours, 30 minutes
Panama City – FL – 2 hours

Points of Interest
Challenger Learning Center
FSU Reservation
Goodwood Plantation
Maclay State Gardens
Mary Brogan Museum of Arts and Sciences
Museum of Florida History
Wakulla Springs State Park

Shopping Centers
Governor's Square Mall
Market Square Shopping Center
Tallahassee Mall

Major Sports Teams
Jacksonville Jaguars: football

Movie Theaters
AMC Tallahassee Mall 20
2415 N. Monroe St.
(850) 386-4330

IMAX Theatre
200 S. Duval St.
(850) 645-7827

Regal Miracle 5
1815 Thomasville Rd.
(850) 224-2617

Regal Governor's Square
1501 Governor's Square Blvd.
(850) 878-7211

Student Life Cinema
113 S. Wildwood Dr.
Florida State campus
(850) 644-4455

Did You Know?

5 Fun Facts about Tallahassee:

- Tallahassee is the state capital of Florida.
- It is ranked as the No. 2 medium-sized college city in which to live.
- Tallahassee is considered one of America's most educated cities.
- On any given day, you may run into George Clinton (Parliament), Ted Turner, Jimmy Buffet, or several other celebrities who live in the area.
- The Mary Brogan Museum of Art and Science, also called the MOAS, was formerly known as The Museum of Art and Science and the Odyssey Science Center. The MOAS offers a variety of educational programs, and FSU students have participated in a chemistry magic show. It also encourages student exhibitions, and admission is free to students.

Local Slang:

Fixin' to – Meaning "getting ready to."

I reckon – A Southerner says this meaning "I think that."

Sink – A shortening of "sinkhole." These are fairly popular swimming holes that dot the Apalachicola National Forest south of campus. The water comes from underground springs and is ice cold. These are great for hot August afternoons.

The Strip – The stretch of Tennessee Street near campus that consists of several popular student bars and clubs.

Tennessee Waltz – Hitting all the bars on Tennessee Street in one night. This is usually done in celebration of a 21st birthday, when many of the drinking establishments offer a free beer or pitcher to the celebrant.

Students Speak Out On...
Local Atmosphere

Q Just Right for Me

I practically grew up in Tallahassee... I already know my way around, which makes it that much easier to enjoy the atmosphere

Q Always a Good Time in Tallahassee

Life around FSU's campus is always booming with people and various things going on. Bars and clubs within walking distance to campus have specials everyday of the week. There is always somewhere to go to enjoy a cold drink, or just go out with friends and dance the night away. FSU has great sports teams, so there are sporting events to watch all year. Locals are nice to students, and many will give discounts at their restuarants or shops.

Q Tallahassee - the Perfect College City

I have lived in quite a few big cities in my life, I lived in the Dallas/Ft. Worth Metroplex in Texas for most of my life. They could be rather chaotic, but Tallahassee is the perfect environment for college students. There are three colleges in the city, and it shows. The atmosphere of Tallahassee is one of welcoming energy. There is always something to do, always something going on. I wouldn't pick any other city to go to school at.

Q My School Is Number One

Tallahassee is a true college town. Famous for athletics and lots of fun social events and school pride. Great musical and theatrical talent as well as the other arts.

Q Going Back to Tally? Not a Chore in the Least!

I've lived a block away from the University of Central Florida all of my life but I find the college all-around atmosphere a lot more welcoming in Tallahassee. Given that it's the capital, the capital building is open for tours, a mere 2 streets over you are met with a very large view of almost the entire city, and there are 2 malls within 10minuts from campus. The bars directly off campus are great and the university provides a free bus service (the NightNole) providing for a safe night of drinking if your evening goes into that direction. There are also the blue light emergency poles literally every 200ft on campus and in the case of an emergency, the local police are no more than 30seconds from you. Our football stadium is also fantastic allowing all students to attend our games for free at open seating. I've never been bored at Florida State!

Q Perfect College Town

Although Tallahassee is the capital, so there is a lot going on. It is also the perfect college town. The spirit of the city is undeniable when it comes to supporting the school-- whether it be in community service, sporting events, or academics. It is also such a great college experience to be in a town where the majority of the people you are around are also students or somehow related to the school.

Q Tourist Town

Panama City is a small town, but its starting to gain more attractions besides the beautiful white beaches. Pier Park is the best place for shopping and Wonder Works is the most entertaining place to be when its raining.

Q So Cool

The town has many different parts. There is always something there for students to do. Especially at night. The Strip is where most students go at night. Its really close to the FSU campus and A lot of people enjoy it. They have everything you can look for in a city. There's always something you can do there. Its awesome.

The College Prowler Take On...
Local Atmosphere

This is a Southern town, so expect things to move at a slower pace. However, don't be fooled into thinking that nothing happens here. During the spring and summer, the state legislature is in session and the town is filled with movers and shakers. For political science, business, and communications majors, this can give the opportunity to see the deal-making and schmoozing first-hand. As for students that do not have an interest in government or legislation, there is still a lot to do in Tallahassee.

Tallahassee is home to two universities and a community college, so there is a large student population present, and not with just FSU students. This means there are twice as many bars, parties, and other activities to keep the average student entertained. More intellectual pursuits are also available in the form of museums, nature trails, and archeological sites. For the more adventurous, there are numerous places to visit that are within a few hours drive of town, including Wakulla Springs, the Florida Caverns, and the Gulf Specimen Marine Lab. Students also like to go to Panama City where the culture is very eclectic. Just keep in mind that appearances can be deceiving, and there is more to do in Tallahassee than meets the eye.

The College Prowler® Grade on

Local
Atmosphere: B+

A high Local Atmosphere grade indicates that the area surrounding campus is safe and scenic. Other factors include nearby attractions, proximity to other schools, and the town's attitude toward students.

Health & Safety

The Lowdown On...
Health & Safety

Security Office
FSU Police Department
830 W. Jefferson St.
(850) 644-1234
www.police.fsu.edu

Safety Services
Crime alerts
Emergency phones
Personal property registration
Rape Aggression Defense
(RAD)
S.A.F.E. Escort Service

SafeBus
Silent Witness
Victim advocacy program

Crimes on Campus
Aggravated Assault: 20
Arson: 8
Burglary: 61
Murder/Manslaughter: 0
Robbery: 8
Sex Offenses: 6
Vehicle Theft: 18

Health Center
Thagard Student Health Center
Magnolia Way, near Montgomery Gym
(850) 644-6230
www.tshc.fsu.edu
Monday–Friday 8 a.m.–4 p.m.

Health Services
Allergy care
Immunizations
Laboratory
Pharmacy
Physical therapy
Primary care
Psychiatry
STD/HIV testing
Travel clinic
Women's health
X-ray

Day Care Services?
Yes

Did You Know?

Confidential mental health counseling is available at no charge to students at the Thagard Student Health Center. Counselors specialize in many different areas, including alcohol/drug abuse, anger, assault/date rape, assertiveness, anxiety, depression, discrimination, eating disorders, family, grief, relationships, self-esteem, sexual abuse, sexuality/sexual orientation, social isolation, stress, suicidal thoughts, test anxiety/study skills, and time management. Counseling options include individual counseling, group counseling, couples counseling, crisis intervention, referrals, psychiatric consultation, workshops and presentations, and peer-facilitation training.

Students Speak Out On...
Health & Safety

ℚ Very Safe

You will feel totally safe on campus. There are emergency pylons all over campus that will alert the campus police if you're in danger. There's also a nightly cab service for campus only that's free and will get you from one place to the next, just in case you're still not feeling safe. The campus authorities also email announcements to every student if there was a crime or assault in a nearby area along with instructions on what to do if you were ever in the same situation.

ℚ Safety of the Campus

Since I live off-campus, I don't really know about the campus crimes, but the campus police force has the cellphone numbers of every student as well as the email addresses so that if there is a crime everyone is told in a mass email. This do with even with the off-campus crimes. This isn't just campus security. This is a police force like in any other part of the city. The police force for the university only rages in the hundreds and every day of the week at any time of the day you can see them riding around through the campus and students. I actually feel pretty safe with all the measures they take to keep the student body safe from crimes. At any time of the night, if one doesn't feel safe to walk through the campus, all we have to do is call them at their number and they will give us a ride to the place where we have to go. It doesn't matter if we live off-campus or on. It's a really safe campus. No late night pranks and the police always keep an eye on the student body.

Q Florida State Is Secure and Safe.

Students receive text alerts to the cell phones when there is an incident that could affect the students. Campus police are visible all around campus as well as emergency poles placed very conveniently. and the campus is well lit at night.

Q Apparently Safe

I am a distance learner so I cannot know for sure about the safety of FSU's campus. Nonetheless, the university does send out text message and email emergency notices when there is a perceived danger.

Q Safe Environment

Dont know of any safety issue on campus. It actually feels safe and peaceful. I personally dont feel threaten and feel safe to walk anywhere at anytime.

Q Florida State Review

Dedicated campus police ensure that the campus is safe at all times and respond promptly if a situation does arise.

Q Good Security Measures

The pathways are well-lit, and every few feet there is a safety emergency pole in case you need assistance. They send out FSU Alerts any time there is a need for students to know of emergency situations. However, I would not advise going out late at night because despite all these measures there are people who might mess with you as emails have proven. Just use common sense and you should be safe.

Q Safe Place

tallahassee is a very safe city, and not much dangerous happens on campus. there have been isolated incedents.

The College Prowler Take On...
Health & Safety

Perhaps because Tallahasee is such a friendly town, people tend to take for granted that serious crimes rarely ever happen. Still, the University's Office of Safety and Security has done everything possible to ensure that the campus is extremely safe. Emergency phones are attached to blue light posts all around campus and the Safety and Security Shuttle allows students who feel either unsafe to walk or are too inebriated to drive from running into trouble. Most female students admit to feeling very safe when they walk across campus late at night, especially because all paths and streets tend to be well lit and clear of huge bushes or trees. All dorms require ID cards to enter, and as a result, many students don't always feel the need to lock their doors.

One of the main problems that occurs on campus is theft, mostly in places like Strozier Library or the Student Life Building, where students often leave their belongings unattended for long periods of time. Safety and Security officers generally do a very good job of tracking down stolen items, and for the most part, students tend not to steal from other students. Even so, Safety and Security encourages students to register their bicycles with the school in case they are stolen and then turn up a week later somewhere in town—as has been known to happen before.

The College Prowler® Grade on

Health & Safety: C+

A high grade in Health & Safety means that students generally feel safe, campus police are visible, blue-light phones and escort services are readily available, and safety precautions are not overly necessary.

Computers

The Lowdown On...
Computers

Wireless Access
Yes: Libraries, most classroom buildings, Wildwood and DeGraff dorms

24-Hour Labs?
No

Charged to Print?
Yes: 5 cents a page

Special Software & Hardware Discounts

Student discounts are offered at campus bookstores. Plenty of discounted software is available from Adobe, Microsoft, Apple, SAS, Corel, SPSS, Sun, McAfee, and other companies.

Did You Know?

 Yahoo! ranked FSU as the 18th most wired university in the nation.

Students Speak Out On...
Computers

ℚ No Worries the Library Has It Minus Finals and Midterms

My school provides laptop if you happen to forget yours or do not have one. There is a Starbucks in the library. It actually feels like a college style Barnes and Noble. Some one is always there to help you and everything is fair.

ℚ Fsview

i really do like the computers at FSU. The are quick and reliable. I have been known to take advantage of the computers to do homework and catch up on some readying. The best thing is that there are so many of them that you can always find a spare computer if you need one.

ℚ Great New Computer Lab

The new computer lab in the library is excellent. The computers are very new, the internet speed is fast, and there are an abundance for the hectic midterm season.

ℚ Computer Labs Are Pretty Convenient

Almost every building has wireless internet and have places to sit with outlets, which is nice inbetween classes if you have your laptop and can't make it to the library. There are also several computer labs around campus, you just have to know where they are (strozier, the union, the science library..)

ℚ FSU College of Engineering

There are 3 computer labs on campus as well as computers around the building so you can almost always find a computer to use. Also, everyone has there own account so saving important files, projects, and printing out documents makes it more convenient.

Q Personal Computer
I prefer to use my personal computer and I am able to use it very efficiently.

Q The Computers Are Pretty Good There.
As is to be expected, the computers at uni only really get crowded and are used the most during exam weeks, which also slows down the wireless networks just about everywhere. The internet connections in the dorms, though, are pretty amazing.

Q Computers Are Available Most of the Time
There is usually no issues when looking for a computer during midterms and finals, but they are crowded. So, if you are part of a group it would be difficult to find space for everyone to sit together during midterms and finals. But with the WiFi bringing your own laptop can definitely help.

The College Prowler Take On...
Computers

Florida State University prides itself on being one of the most wired universities in the United States. The administration realizes that in order to be competitive, students must have access to the latest technologies. FSU is constantly updating their computer systems and network servers, not only for security purposes, but also to provide its student body with the most up-to-date computing available and the quickest network speed possible. This includes Ethernet connections and wired classrooms, along with a wireless network available at various locations. Many instructors now use FSU's Blackboard system to post class notes, assignments, and grades that are easy for students to access from any computer location, regardless if you own one or not.

Some students complain about crowded computer labs, but these are usually the ones who wait until the last minute to complete their assignments. Also, the school has adopted a stricter policy on file trading due to the strain it puts on the network servers and to avoid the possibility of copyright infringement lawsuits. This new enforcement helps to speed up the network. In addition to these new policies, the systems have been upgraded, continuing to make the network quicker. Having your own computer is not a necessity at FSU, but it is nice to have the convenience of checking your e-mail or communicating via Instant Messenger in the comfort of your own room.

B

The College Prowler® Grade on

Computers: B

A high grade in Computers designates that computer labs are available, the computer network is easily accessible, and the campus's computing technology is up-to-date.

Facilities

The Lowdown On...
Facilities

Campus Size
395 acres

Student Centers
The Student Life Building

Main Libraries
Allen Music Library
Dirac Science Library
Goldstein Library of Science
Ringling Museum of
Art Library
Strozier Library

Service & Maintenance Staff
598

Popular Places to Chill
Landis Green
Oglesby Union
Starbucks

Bar on Campus

Chili's in the Oglesby Union includes a full bar
Club Downunder in Oglesby Union

Bowling on Campus

Crenshaw Lanes is located in the Oglesby Union

Coffeehouse on Campus

A full-service Starbucks is located on Learning Way, on the West side of campus.

Movie Theater on Campus

There is a movie theater in the Student Life Building, and it's free for students. In addition to the latest new releases and a mix of older films, the SLB Theatre also holds special screenings of FSU Film School projects and independent films.

Favorite Things To Do

The choices of activities are limited if you don't have a car. The Student Activities Office does a great job of offering activities for students at little or no cost for weekend activities. Without a car, many students visit the local Sheetz. With a car, Monaca is only a 15-minute drive, where Beaver Valley Mall, movies, restaurants, and plenty more can be found. Also, Chippewa is only five minutes away, with a Wal-Mart, some restaurants, and Sal's, a popular bar for Geneva students. Some more popular events from Student Activities are the Mystery Bus Trips, Fall Fest, Midnight Madness, the Big Event, Big Bad, Big Wheel Rally, Midnight Breakfast, and Homecoming Weekend.
With so many options of things to do on campus, it would be difficult to pin down specific favorites, but the majority of students enjoy breaking a sweat at the Leach Center, swimming, catching a movie at the SLB, or hanging out at Oblesby Union.
You can spend your free time taking in a movie, working out at the Leach Center, swimming, or bowling at the Student Union. In addition to that, there are usually visiting speakers, plays, live music, and a weekly flea market on campus at any

given time. Several times during the year, you can catch the FSU Flying High Circus under the big top next to Dick Howser Stadium.

Did You Know?

The Tallahassee Democrat noted that the Westcott building is the oldest site of higher education in Florida.

Students Speak Out On...
Facilities

Q Libraries

The libraries at Florida State are great. One of them is open 24 hours druing the week, it offers free tutoring for students, there's plenty of computers, printers and copiers. It is very convenient to study in groups or alone, since there is sudy rooms available too.

Q There Is Everything on This Campus from State of the Art Labs to a Circus!

The whole campus at Florida State University is gorgeous. The campus is enormous and kept very pristeen. The University is known for it's education, football and party atmospere!

Q Main Library Is Amazing!

They have recently renewed the main library of the school,and it is amazing! The first floor is so comfortable because it includes booths, tables and individual chairs that come with built in desks but have the comfortability of a couch! It's soo comfortable to relax and socialize or study vigorously for an exam. They also offer Smart rooms which are private study rooms equipped with the Smart Board and the other wall of the room is either an entire whiteboard or a chalkboard.

Q They Have a Theater

Florida State has an on campus movie theater where students can watch new and classic movies for free. It has it's own website so we can check on what's playing on any given night, and it has a concession stand. It has everything a theater should and it's staffed by students as a way to provide more jobs.

ⵕ There Is Nothing Like Florida State

Everything at Florida State's campus is just beautiful. Every day you walk around campus and could not be happier with everything around you. Everyone is kind and willing to help you, including other students. The gym has everything you could ask for (but could get crowded at times), the libraries are being renovated and look great and are as full functioning as you could ever ask for. The social life is the best in the country, and if you deny it, just spend a weekend here at FSU. There is nothing like Florida State University, nothing like it in the whole world.

ⵕ Florida State the Most Beautiful Campus in Florida

Florida State University has the most attractive college campus in the state of Florida in my opinion. The hills that the campus is built on remind me of the foothills of northern Georgia and there are trees everywhere. Some college campuses are built with trendy architecture styles but Florida State is mostly brick buildings that are beautiful and can stand the test of time.

ⵕ Campus

The facilities are amazing on campus. Everything is almost brand new and the people are always very friendly.

ⵕ Libraries

The newly renovated Strozier Library is the new hot spot to study in. Thanks to Florida State University Student Government Association, there are new computers and study areas, a convenient 24/5 starbucks and more space to study for exams or tests.

The College Prowler Take On...
Facilities

FSU has been actively remodeling and renovating older buildings on campus, as well as providing students with modern entertainment venues. You don't have to worry if you don't have transportation because you can always find something to do around campus. The students who complain that there is nothing to do on campus are the ones who never leave their dorm rooms. At a school like FSU that offers an abundance of things to do, you have to try pretty hard to be bored.

The Student Life Building, which was recently completed, boasts a movie theater (showing a number of new releases each semester) and a Cyber Café. If exercise is more your style, then the Leach Recreation Center and Stults Aquatic Center are great places to break a sweat and check out the talent. Early mornings and late evenings are the best times to go if you're serious about working out. The exercise equipment and pool are well maintained, and there is usually someone on staff around to provide assistance should the need arise. The Student Union offers Club Downunder (which brings in live music on a regular basis), a bowling alley, game room, as well as eating establishments, a barbershop, and a weekly flea market. Entertainment is also occasionally provided by a mix of public speakers who are unashamed to stand up and spout their views, which generally leads to an interesting exchange of ideas between speaker and audience. A lot goes on in the new Student Life Building, so it's a popular place for students to go for entertainment; however it's not the only entertainment facility that FSU offers.

B+

The College Prowler® Grade on
Facilities: B+

A high Facilities grade indicates that the campus is aesthetically pleasing and well-maintained; facilities are state-of-the-art, and libraries are exceptional. Other determining factors include the quality of both athletic and student centers and an abundance of things to do on campus.

Campus Dining

The Lowdown On...
Campus Dining

Average Meal Plan Cost
$3200 per year

Freshman Meal Plan Required?
Yes: Meal plans are required in certain residence halls.

24-Hour Dining
Park Avenue Diner

Dining Halls & Campus Restaurants

Barrister's Bistro
Location: College of Law
Food: Sandwiches, coffee
Hours: Monday–Friday 7:30 a.m.–2 p.m.

Chili's
Location: Oglesby Union Food Court
Food: American
Hours: Monday–Thursday 10:30 a.m.–11 p.m., Friday 10:30 a.m.-12 a.m., Saturday 12 p.m.–12 a.m., Sunday 12 p.m.–11 p.m.

Einstein Bros. Bagels
Location: Oglesby Union Food Court
Food: Bagels, sandwiches
Hours: Monday–Thursday 7 a.m.–4 p.m., Friday 7 a.m.–3 p.m.

The Figg Player's Dining Room
Location: Coyle Moore
Food: All-you-can-eat lunch
Hours: Monday–Friday 11 a.m.–1:30 p.m.

The Fresh Food Company
Location: West side of campus, next to McCollum Hall
Food: All-you-can-eat entrees, salads, soups
Hours: Monday–Thursday 7:30 a.m.–10 p.m., Friday 7:30 a.m.–7:30 p.m., Saturday 10:30 a.m.–7:30 p.m., Sunday 10:30 a.m.–10 p.m.

Hardee's
Location: Oglesby Union Food Court
Food: Fast food
Hours: Monday–Thursday 7:30 a.m.–4 p.m., Friday 7:30 a.m.–3 p.m.

Miso
Location: Oglesby Union Food Court
Food: Salads, stir fry, wraps
Hours: Monday–Friday 10:30 a.m.–3 p.m.

Park Avenue Diner
Location: Student Services Building
Food: Diner fare, like breakfast, burgers, melts, milkshakes, sandwiches
Hours: Daily 24 hours

Pollo Tropical
Location: Oglesby Union Food Court
Food: Chicken, rice, beans, hearty sides
Hours: Monday–Thursday 10:30 a.m.–7 p.m., Friday 10:30 a.m.-4 p.m.

Quiznos Subs
Location: Oglesby Union Food Court
Food: Bagels, sandwiches

Hours: Monday–Thursday
10:30 a.m.–7 p.m., Friday
10:30 a.m.–5 p.m.

Starbucks
Location: FSU bookstore
Food: Coffee
Hours: Monday–Thursday 8
a.m.–3 p.m., Friday 8 a.m.–2
p.m.

Starbucks
Location: 977 Learning Way
Food: Coffee, salads,
sandwiches
Hours: Monday–Thursday
6:30 a.m.–10 p.m.,
Friday 6:30 a.m.–8 p.m.,
Saturday–Sunday 10 a.m.–8
p.m.

Starbucks
Location: Strozier Library
Food: Coffee
Hours: Monday–Thursday 8
a.m.–12 a.m., Friday 8 a.m.–4
p.m.

The Suwannee Room
Location: William Johnston
Building
Food: All-you-can-eat
Hours: Monday–Thursday
7:30 a.m.–10 p.m., Friday
7:30 a.m.–7:30 p.m.,
Saturday 10:30 a.m.–7:30
p.m., Sunday 10:30 a.m.–10
p.m.

The Trading Post
Location: Oglesby Union
Food Court

Food: Convenience items,
hot dogs, pizza, grab 'n go
Hours: Monday–Thursday
7:30 a.m.–7 p.m., Friday 7:30
a.m.–5 p.m.

Student Favorites

Einstein Bros. Bagels

Suwannee Room

Off-Campus Places to Use Flex Money

None

Did You Know?

In addition to the main Starbucks locations, carts can be found at various locations throughout campus, although most aren't open late.

Many students love that the renovated Suwannee Room closely resembles the Great Hall from the Harry Potter movies and novels.

Students Speak Out On...
Campus Dining

Q Eating Like a Seminole

There are plenty of delicious options and varieties to choose from on the great campus of Florida State. Not only are the dining halls full of numerous options, there are also resturants right in the middle of campus! Chilis, Hardees, Pollo Tropical are just to name a few. The campus also features 2 Starbucks, all of which you can use your flex bucks at. There's also a Diner that is open 24 hours, which always stays busy and full of hungry students just waiting to be satisfied.

Q From Original to Chain

FSU has the best situation when it comes to o campus dining. There is a starbucks cafe right in the library. The union has chain restaurants such as chilis and Hardies. My favorite place to eat on campus is the 60's diner that serves, quite possibly, the best burger in town.

Q Great, Just Eat in Moderation

The dining is great! I enjoy every meal, but if you eat there all the time, you won't have many other options except for outside the school.

Q Best Campus Dining Experience

I have gone to several different schools for visits, and Florida State had by far the best dining options. There are two dining halls located on campus, which offer a very wide variety of foods, all fresh and delicious. Being a vegetarian I thought it would be very hard to find food that I would be able to eat, but not at FSU! There are specific counters in each dining hall that offer vegetarian and vegan food, which I found absolutley amazing, they sold me at that! The food is always delicious and is never greasy or overly fried, I eat there twice a day, and I love it!

Q FSU's Yum Yums
Both dining halls are always filled with a variety of food to choose from whether you are a meat lover, vegetarian, or health-addict. The facilities are well-sized and always clean; there are always employees available for your service. The other food places are located conveniently around campus near ATM's and serve high-quality food as if you were buying off campus. I would recommend a meal plan to anyone attending FSU.

Q Dining Halls
the dining halls on campus are wonderful and offer a variety of food everyday. everyone has an option of something to eat no matter what they like. it is not to expensive and if you dont use all your money in the dining halls you can use them all over campus which is very helpful.

Q Alright, but Bland
The dining halls are conveniently placed, but the food leaves a little to be desired.

Q Ok but Very Repetitve
I like eating on campus but its too similar to eat every day for every meal. it is convenient though.

The College Prowler Take On...
Campus Dining

Most students will complain about on campus dining, but ironically, the restaurants and dining halls are usually busy. The loudest complaints are often from underclassmen who are still adjusting to not having a home-cooked meal every night. Upperclassmen will grumble about the food, because they eat it all the time. They'll eat it, still, mostly out of convenience. Many of the establishments are open late, which is a plus for night owls and late-night revelers. The meal plans get mixed reviews. Students who are just looking for fuel to get through the day would probably do well with a meal plan due to a few buffet-style dining halls and all-you-can-eat options. For those who just grab a quick bite between classes or are interested in healthy dining, you would be better off venturing off campus or waiting for the next care package from home.

The food scene on campus has been steadily improving over the past several years, offering more choices and better quality than in the past. But still, it is cafeteria food and in no way can compare to the food your mom makes at home. You won't starve, but you won't be amazed, either. There are also several vendors who pop up on campus around lunch time who offer the obligatory hot dogs, chips, and soda, which can come in handy if you need a quick bite while hustling to your next class.

B-

The College Prowler® Grade on
Campus Dining: B-

The grade on Campus Dining addresses the quality of both school-owned dining halls and independent on-campus restaurants as well as the price, availability, and variety of food.

Off-Campus Dining

The Lowdown On...
Off-Campus Dining

Restaurant Listings

4th Quarter Bar & Grill
Food: American
2033 N. Monroe St.
(850) 385-0017
Price: $8–$12

Andrew's Capital Bar & Grill
Food: American
228 S. Adams St.
(850) 222-3444
www.andrewsdowntown.com/capitalgrill.html
Price: $10–$18

Bagel Bagel
Food: Bagels
2401 W. Pensacola St.
(850) 574-1814
www.bagelbagelcafe.com
Price: $2–$8

Bella Bella
Food: Italian
123 E. 5th Ave.
(850) 412-1114
www.bellabellatallahassee.com
Price: $10–$25

Black Dog Café
Food: Coffee, pastries
229 Lake Ella Dr.
(850) 224-2518
Price: $5–$8

China Super Buffet
Food: Chinese
2698 N. Monroe St.
(850) 553-9292
Price: $5–$10

Cici's Pizza
Food: Pizza
800 Ocala Rd.
(850) 580-2424
www.cicispizza.com
Price: $6–$10

The Crepevine
Food: Crepes
2020 W. Pensacola St.
(850) 562-7373
www.thecrepevine.com
Price: $5–$10

Gordo's
Food: Cuban
1907 W. Pensacola St.
(850) 576-5767
www.gordoscubanfood.com
Price: $5–$12

Gumby's Pizza
Food: Pizza
623 W. Tennessee St.
(850) 224-8629
www.gumbyspizza.com
Price: $5–$10

Hopkins' Eatery
Food: Healthy/sandwiches
1840 N. Monroe St.
(850) 386-4258
www.hopkinseatery.com
Price: $5–$8

Jim & Milt's Bar-B-Q
Food: American/Southern
1923 W. Pensacola St.
(850) 576-3998
Price: $6–$10

The Main Ingredient
Food: Multicultural,
vegetarian, mix-and-match
menu
1710 W. Tharpe St.
(850) 383-8333
Price: $10–$15

Mellow Mushroom
Food: Pizza
1641 W. Pensacola St.
(850) 575-0050
www.mellowmushroom.com
Price: $5–$10

Momo's Pizza
Food: Italian
1416 W. Tennessee St.
(850) 224-9808
www.momospizza.com
Price: $4–$8

New Leaf Market & Deli
Food: Sandwiches, salads
1235 Apalachee Parkway
(850) 942-2557
www.newleafmarket.coop
Price: $5–$8

Po' Boys Creole Café

Food: Creole/American
1944 W. Pensacola St.
(850) 224-5400
www.poboys.com
Price: $5–$10

The Rice Bowl

Food: Oriental
3813 N. Monroe St.
(850) 514-3632
Price: $6–$12

TGI Friday's

Food: American
3390 Capital Circle NE
(904) 721-2200
www.tgifridays.com
Price: $8–$15

Torrey's Neighborhood Grill

Food: American
1415 Timberlane Rd.
(850) 893-0326
Price: $10–$15

Waffle House

Food: American
1939 W. Tennessee St.
(850) 224-4922
www.wafflehouse.com
Price: $5–$8

WingZone

Food: Wings
2037 W. Pensacola St.
(850) 576-9464
www.wingzone.com
Price: $5–$10

Best Asian
China Super Buffet

Best Breakfast
Waffle House

Best Healthy
The Crepe Vine

Best Pizza
Gumby's Pizza

Best Wings
WingZone

Best Place to Take Your Parents
Bella Bella

24-Hour Dining
Waffle House

Other Places to Check Out
Applebee's
Bennigan's
Cabarra's
Calico Jack's
Chez Pierre
Chili's
Food Glorious Food
Guthrie's
Hooters
The Loop
The Melting Pot
Olive Garden Italian

Restaurant
On the Border
Ruby Tuesday's

Grocery Stores
Publix Super Market
800 Ocala Rd.
(850) 575-3929

Winn Dixie
1625 W. Tharpe St.
(850) 297-2555

Students Speak Out On...
Off-Campus Dining

Q Culture Clash

There are a variety of ethnic cuisine restaurants in the area surrounding the Florida State Campus. There are Mexican, Colombian, Cuban, Italian, Japanese, and even Indian restaurants in the area. All of the restaurants are also reasonably priced for students and most even have "Student Discount Nights". It definitely keeps my taste buds from dying of boredom from the typical PB & J sandwich, it's great!

Q Taste of Tallahassee

Some of my favorite places to eat in Tallahassee are Mo-Mo's Pizza, Mr. Robotos, and Crape Vine. Of course there is all the fast food places too. Mo-Mo's slices are huge! they cost 3.25 for a slice plus 0.75 for additional toppings. Mr Robotos has delicious hibachi chicken and is about $7 for a plate with salad and rice. Crape Vine is a little pricey but tastes so good, just bring a coupon when you go. The coupon books from bills has discounts for lots of places to try around Tallahassee.

Q So Many Options!

There is food EVERYWHERE in Tallahassee and so much variety! A lot of the restaurants are student friendly in terms of their prices and offer lots of student discounts and coupons. My favorite places are the Crepe Vine, Monks, Gordo's, Mellow Mushroom, and Five Guys. There's every type of cuisine you can imagine. There are also options for fine dining if you are up with your family.

Mr Roboto

One of the restaurants we have thats only in Tallahassee is Mr Roboto, its a sort of fast food sushi/hibachi place and it is sooo good!! Its also priced very well and they have this sauce, called yum-yum sauce that students are crazy for.

Off Campus

The dining options are diverse. They are often open late and have good costs for students.

Lots of Delivery!

Almost every place delivers, which is really great. Some places can be a little more pricey than others, but there are plenty of options (not just pizza.) Most places are college student budget friendly, you can find coupons all over the place. I'd say some of the better restaurants are west of campus, on Pensacola St. & W Tennessee

Good, Lots of Choices

There's alot of fastfood places and restaurants in the Town Center close to the campus. The prices there are affordable and the service is good.

TONS of Restaurants Around Town

There are a ton of restaurants immediately off campus, especially on Tennessee and Pensacola, which are the two roads that go right next to campus on either side. Within walking distance of the school is Chipotle, Ruby Tuesday's, Whattaburger, Jimmy John's, Panda Express, Subway, Sumo Sabi, and a bunch of other places. If you go to Appalachee - about a ten minute drive when there's no traffic, there's a Chili's, Logan's, Outback, Genghis Grill, Olive Garden, etc. And there is a TON of frozen yogurt places around.

The College Prowler Take On...
Off-Campus Dining

It doesn't take long for the call of off-campus food to be heard by the student body at Florida State. There are upwards of 20 restaurants within a five-minute walk off-campus, and these establishments offer a variety of food to choose from. Pizza, buffalo wings, and subs are the most popular choices, but for the more adventurous student a cornucopia of food awaits. Off-campus food selections run the gamut, from pitas and tacos, to gyros and seafood. There are also several vegetarian restaurants if you prefer a greener existence. Remember, Tallahassee is a two-college town, and this means twice as many restaurants to try. However, it is also a political town, and the farther you travel from campus, the more money you are likely to spend on food. To keep it within budget, most students stick close to campus where the dining is cheap and plentiful. Like any good college town, Tallahassee has an army of both locally-owned and chain restaurants encircling the University. The chain restaurants and fast food joints give you just what you expect, and most are within walking distance of the residence halls. The locally-owned establishments can be hit and miss, but if you do find a place that knocks your socks off, enjoy it while you can.

Word travels fast here, and it doesn't take long for a quiet little restaurant to become a standing-room-only, 30-minute-wait madhouse. The Loop, which is right on the edge of campus, is always a good choice for pizza and other Italian specialties. The Main Ingredient can blow you away with its constantly-changing menu and inventive daily specials. Most places are affordable on a student budget, but the farther from campus you go, the higher the prices.

B+

The College Prowler® Grade on

Off-Campus
Dining: B+

A high Off-Campus Dining grade implies that off-campus restaurants are affordable, accessible, and worth visiting. Other factors include the variety of cuisine and the availability of alternative options (vegetarian, vegan, kosher).

Campus
Housing

The Lowdown On...
Campus Housing

On-Campus Housing Available?
Yes

Campus Housing Capacity
7,100

Average Housing Costs
$4,800

Number of Dormitories
14

Number of Campus-Owned Apartments
2

Dormitories

Broward Hall
Floors: 4
Number of Occupants: 135
Bathrooms: Suite-style
Coed: Yes
Residents: Freshmen and upperclassmen
Room Types: Suites (singles, doubles)
Special Features: Community kitchens, ice machine, in-room sink, laundry facilities, moveable furniture, rec room, self-regulated visitation, study lounges, TV lounge, vending machines; meal plan required.

Bryan Hall
Floors: 3
Number of Occupants: 131
Bathrooms: Suite-style
Coed: Yes
Residents: Freshmen
Room Types: Suites (doubles, triples)
Special Features: Community kitchens, ice machine, in-room sinks, laundry facilities, moveable furniture, rec room, self-regulated visitation, study lounges, TV lounge, vending machines; meal plan required. Home to Bryan Hall Learning Community for freshmen.

Cawthon Hall
Floors: 4
Number of Occupants: 297
Bathrooms: Suite-style
Coed: Yes
Residents: Freshmen and upperclassmen
Room Types: Suites (singles, doubles, triples)
Special Features: Community kitchens, computer lab, ice machine, in-room sinks, laundry facilities, moveable furniture, patio, piano, rec room, self-regulated visitation, study lounges, TV lounge, vending machines; meal plan required. Home to Music Living-Learning Center and Women in Math, Science, and Engineering Learning Community.

DeGraff Hall
Floors: 5
Number of Occupants: 700
Bathrooms: Suite-style
Coed: Yes
Residents: Freshmen and upperclassmen
Room Types: Suites (doubles)
Special Features: Community kitchens, ice machine, in-room sinks, laundry facilities, moveable furniture, rec room, self-regulated visitation, study lounges, TV lounge, vending machines; meal plan optional. Home to Social Sciene and Public Affairs Learning Community.

Deviney Hall
Floors: 7
Number of Occupants: 243
Bathrooms: Communal
Coed: Yes
Residents: Freshmen and
upperclassmen
Room Types: Singles,
doubles
Special Features: Community
kitchens, ice machine,
laundry facilities, limited
visitation, moveable
furniture, patio, rec room,
study lounges, TV lounge,
vending machines; meal plan
optional.

Dorman Hall
Floors: 8
Number of Occupants: 276
Bathrooms: Communal
Coed: Yes
Residents: Freshmen and
upperclassmen
Room Types: Singles,
doubles
Special Features: Community
kitchens, ice machine,
laundry facilities, limited
visitation, moveable
furniture, patio, rec room,
study lounges, TV lounge,
vending machines; meal plan
optional.

Gilchrist Hall
Floors: 4
Number of Occupants: 229
Bathrooms: Suite-style
Coed: Yes

Residents: Freshmen and
upperclassmen
Room Types: Suites (singles,
doubles, triples)
Special Features: Community
kitchens, ice machine,
in-room sinks, laundry
facilities, moveable furniture,
rec room, self-regulated
visitation, study lounges, TV
lounge, vending machines;
meal plan required.

Jennie Murphree Hall
Floors: 5
Number of Occupants: 326
Bathrooms: Suite-style
Coed: No, women only
Residents: Freshmen and
upperclassmen
Room Types: Suites (singles,
doubles, triples, quads)
Special Features: Community
kitchens, ice machine,
in-room sinks, laundry
facilities, limited visitation,
moveable furniture, rec room,
study lounges, TV lounge,
vending machines; meal plan
required.

Kellum Hall
Floors: 10
Number of Occupants: 538
Bathrooms: Communal
Coed: Yes
Residents: Freshmen and
upperclassmen
Room Types: Doubles
Special Features: Built-in
furniture, community

kitchens, ice machine, in-room sinks, laundry facilities, limited visitation, rec room, study lounges, TV lounge, vending machines; meal plan optional.

Landis Hall
Floors: 4
Number of Occupants: 402
Bathrooms: Suite-style
Coed: Yes
Residents: Honors Community
Room Types: Suites (singles, doubles, triples, quads)
Special Features: Community kitchens, ice machine, in-room sinks, laundry facilities, moveable furniture, rec room, self-regulated visitation, study lounges, TV lounge, vending machines; meal plan required.

Reynolds Hall
Floors: 3
Number of Occupants: 243
Bathrooms: Suite-style
Coed: Yes
Residents: Freshmen and upperclassmen
Room Types: Suites (singles, doubles, triples)
Special Features: Community kitchens, ice machine, in-room sinks, laundry facilities, moveable furniture, rec room, self-regulated visitation, study lounges, TV lounge, vending machines;

meal plan required. Home to Wellness Lifestyle Program and Pre-Health Professions Learning Community.

Salley Hall
Floors: 8
Number of Occupants: 570
Bathrooms: Suite-style
Coed: Yes
Residents: Freshmen and upperclassmen
Room Types: Suites (doubles)
Special Features: Community kitchens, ice machine, laundry facilities, moveable furniture, rec room, self-regulated visitation, study lounges, TV lounge, vending machines; meal plan not required.

Smith Hall
Floors: 9
Number of Occupants: 553
Bathrooms: Communal
Coed: Yes
Residents: Freshmen and upperclassmen
Room Types: Doubles
Special Features: Built-in furniture, community kitchens, computer lab, ice machine, in-room sinks, laundry facilities, limited visitation, rec room, study lounges, TV lounge, vending machines; meal plan optional.

Wildwood Hall

Floors: 5
Number of Occupants: 700
Bathrooms: Suite-style
Coed: Yes
Residents: Freshmen and upperclassmen
Room Types: Suites (doubles)
Special Features: Community kitchens, ice machine, in-room sinks, laundry facilities, moveable furniture, rec room, self-regulated visitation, study lounges, TV lounge, vending machines; meal plan optional. Home to Nursing and Social Justice learning communities.

Ragans Hall

Floors: 5
Number of Units: 140
Bathrooms: Private
Coed: Yes
Residents: Upperclassmen
Room Types: Four-bedroom apartments (singles)
Utilities included in rent.
Special Features: Ice machine, laundry facilities, living room and full kitchen in each unit, rec room, self-regulated visitation, TV lounge, vending machines; meal plan optional.

Campus-Owned Apartments

McCollum Hall

Floors: 6
Number of Units: 199 students
Bathrooms: Private
Coed: Yes
Residents: Upperclassmen
Room Types: Efficiencies (singles), two-bedroom apartments (doubles)
Special Features: Air conditioning, ice machine, laundry facilities, living/ dining rooms and full kitchen in each unit, rec room, self-regulated visitation, TV lounge, vending machines; meal plan optional.

Undergrads Living On Campus
19%

Best Dorms
Broward Hall
Gilchrist Hall
Reynolds Hall

Worst Dorms
Dorman Hall
Salley Hall
Smith Hall

What You Get
Bed
Closet
Desk and chair
Dresser
Ethernet connection
Free local phone calls
Security-card access
Small refrigerator

Did You Know?

Many of the dormitories are said to be "haunted," and Cawthon Hall has a haunted house for students to walk through on Halloween night.

Suites offer semi-private baths. There are two kinds of apartments offered. Efficiency apartments are one-bedroom apartments, and townhouse apartments have four bedrooms. Computer connections are offered in every dormitory. Television rooms, kitchens, recreational rooms, and laundry rooms can be found in every residence hall, as well.

Students Speak Out On...
Campus Housing

ℚ Summary

THE COLLEGE DORMS ARE AWESOME... a GREAT ROOM AND EVEN SO MANY GREAT PEOPLE AROUND YOU. tHE ATMOSPHERE OVERALL IS GREAT!!!

ℚ Honors College Dorms Are the Best!!

At FSU, on-campus housing comes on a first-come, first-served basis. Typically, freshman are stuck in the bad dorms of Smith and Kellum. But there are a special group of kids that get to live in Landis, which is one of the best dorms on campus. It's clean and right across from Landis Green, a popular tanning spot.

ℚ It's Awesome!

Living on campus is the best part of FSU. There's always an activity to do and there are an abundance of things that go on throughout the week so it's very easy to socialize and make new friends. The worst part of living on campus is the parking in the afternoon. It's always a struggle.

ℚ Be Social

Living on campus offers a wide variety of opportunities that I found very helpful my first year living outside of the comforts of my parents house. The first thing I noticed about living in a dorm was how fast and easy it was to make new friends. Since you are in so close proximity to others just like you, meeting people is super easy. The next thing I noticed was how helpful it was not having to drive to class everyday. Florida State is a big school and parking can become next to impossible during school hours, so being able to walk to class everyday made it much easier to keep up attendance. The final thing I noticed about living on campus was the availability of the maintenance staff and how friendly they were in assisting my roomate's and my problems. For example, while living in the dorm, our sink had started to constantly drip. One morning I dropped off an information ticket to the front office, went to class, and when I came back, my sink was completely drip free! In conclusion, I think that living on campus is a helpful and rewarding experience, especially for incoming freshman.

Q Living on Campus

I do not live on campus personally, but for all of my friends that do, they say it is very convient. It takes 15 minutes tops to walk from one side of campus to the other. Most of the dorms are in tip top shape, and are actually pretty homey/spacey. Best options include the honors hall, Landis. Worst dorm options include Kellum hall! My friends that live on campus have met a lot of friends this year because of living in dorms.

Q Good

Landis is pretty nice, but check to see if a meal plan is required for your dorm - could be a deciding factor.

Q Campus

amazing experience, beautiful campus, just make sure to get a high priority number so you get a decent dorm, some are very trashy

Q Feels Like Home

I loved living on-campus. I lived in a suite style dorm where I shared a bathroom with 4 other girls. This year I will be living in an upperclassman dorm, which is apartment style.

The College Prowler Take On...
Campus Housing

On-campus housing can be hit-or-miss. A small percentage of students love living on campus where they have all the amenities of home and are close to their classes. Florida State is working hard to renovate the older dormitories and bring them all up to par with the newer facilities, so the new and renovated dorms are very nice, and most are suite-style. The biggest downfall is that many are home to groups that you need to be a part of to live there, and anyone living in the East campus dorms must purchase a meal plan. As far as suggestions go, your best bet is to visit campus and see the dorms for yourself. It doesn't hurt to ask around. Some of the dorms are fairly quiet and are better suited for the heavy studier, while others tend to house the late-night revelers. If nothing else, dorm living is a great way to meet people and make friends. Just remember, don't expect it to be as nice as living at home.

FSU has been refurbishing the dormitories over the last few years, with favorable results. The upgrades include high-speed Internet access and modern conveniences, such as suite-style bathrooms and working elevators. The older dorms are livable, but they're not the kind of places you're going to write home about. They've seen better days, but they aren't project tenaments, by any means. Relying on word-of-mouth is an excellent way to avoid the less-luxurious dorms. If you have no other choice but to stay in a dorm, consider it a learning experience.

The College Prowler® Grade on

Campus Housing: C+

A high Campus Housing grade indicates that dorms are clean, well-maintained, and spacious. Other determining factors include variety of dorms, proximity to classes, and social atmosphere.

Off-Campus Housing

The Lowdown On...
Off-Campus Housing

Undergrads Living Off Campus
81%

Average Off-Campus Room & Board
$8,000

Average Rents
Studio: $389
1 BR: $400
2 BR: $650
4 BR: $1,070

Best Time to Look for a Place
Summer, or at least one month before semester begins

Popular Areas
Downtown
Jackson Bluff
Ocala Road
Pensacola Street

Students Speak Out On...
Off-Campus Housing

ℚ Tallahassee Is a Hub for Off-Campus Living

The city of Tallahassee is filled with apartment complexes to suit any budget and necessity. Many students either live on campus all four years or move off after freshman year. It really just depends on the individual student. The apartment complexes are all shapes and sizes and pretty much any need may be filled in at least one of the complexes around Florida's capital city.

ℚ Off Campus Housing

There are many off campus housing choices here. The best thing about them is that most of them are pretty close to campus. There is sure to be something for every budget.

ℚ Off Campus Housing

I love off-campus housing! Finding an apartment or even a house to rent is super easy! With help from SHS (Student Housing Solutions) you can tell them exactly what you're looking for and they can find it almost immediately. The amenities like free food and pool parties are always a plus, along with the option to pick your roomates or live with randoms. Many apartments are close to campus, if not near a bus stop. Also most apartment leases are separate amongst your room mates, therefore you're not held liable if your roomies dont pay up!

ℚ Living Off Campus Is at Least Better Than Living on Campus

There are a lot of options for off campus living around Florida State's campus. Where I chose to live (which I would rather not name) was a bit expensive compared to where my friend's lived; i payed $485 a month for rent, plus electric for a two bedroom, two bathroom. The apartment I plan on living in next year is much cheaper: $315 plus utilies, but it is also a four bedroom, two bathroom, but it is also much bigger than where I'm living now, as well as closer to campus.

Q Off-Campus Housing

There are tons of aparments and townhouses all over that range from $350-$700/mo. It just depends on where you want to live, if you want to live in a 1/1-4/4. Finding a student apartment is easy and there are so many close to campus. If you don't have a vehicle- no worries there is a city bus that goes to almost every single apartment complex. You just have to know the routes.

Q Living Off-Campus

There are so many options to choose from apartments and houses located near the campus, and the cost depends on proximity to campus and size.I found a house just by driving around looking for places to rent.

Q Off-Campus Housing

There is plenty of housing off campus. From apartments to town homes and even single family homes. a lot of great locations close to campus and a great bus system.

Q Osceola Village and West Ten

Probably two of the best off campus houing options. Osceola is right off campus and West Ten is a very nice, rich looking place too. There are other places off campus that are okay but some that you want to stay away from, these places include Frenchtown apartments or the like .

The College Prowler Take On...
Off-Campus Housing

Many, many students choose to live off-campus. Florida State University is centrally located in Tallahassee, so traveling to and from campus shouldn't be too much of a problem. Over the past few years, at least 20 new apartment complexes have gone up on the outskirts of campus. These newer developments offer amenities such as computer labs, athletic facilities, and gated security. The closer you are to campus, the older and dingier the apartments. Living off-campus can be cheaper than living in a residence hall and can offer you more privacy.

One thing to keep in mind is the City of Tallahassee's Party Patrol. This is a police unit that patrols the residential neighborhoods and responds to party/noise complaints. They are serious about preventing underage drinking and keeping the local residents happy. This doesn't mean you can't enjoy yourself in off-campus housing. You just have to respect your neighbors. Another policy that the Tallahassee City Commission is trying to pass is limiting the number of non-family members living together in a single residence. Since this policy has met with resistance, no action has been taken yet. It is still something to consider, though, if you plan on living off-campus.

B

The College Prowler® Grade on

Off-Campus
Housing: B

A high grade in Off-Campus Housing indicates that apartments are of high quality, close to campus, affordable, and easy to secure.

Diversity

The Lowdown On...
Diversity

African American
11%

Native American
1%

Asian American
3%

White
71%

Hispanic
12%

Unknown
1%

International
1%

Out-of-State Students
9%

Faculty Diversity

African American: 4%
Asian American: 8%
Hispanic: 4%
International: 6%
Native American: 0%
White: 77%
Unknown: 0%

Historically Black College/University?

No

Student Age Breakdown

Under 18: 0%
18-19: 28%
20-21: 36%
22-24: 22%
25+: 14%

Economic Status

You'll hear the usual complaints about "rich kids," and more than a handful of students drive cars you know they didn't pay for themselves. However, the economic status of the student body varies, and FSU does a good job of bringing in students from all walks of life.

Gay Pride

While Florida State is in the south, both the FSU and the local community show a high degree of acceptance for alternative lifestyles and people with different types of sexual orientation. There have been no violent crimes against homosexuals in recent history. The University also hosts the Lesbian/Gay/Bisexual/Transgender Student Union and SafeZone.

Most Common Religions

FSU is mostly Christian, but many other religions are also represented. Many consider Tallahassee to be part of the Bible Belt, and the city plays host to a number of churches.

Political Activity

The most visible political activity on campus, other than student government, is usually activists protesting either real or perceived injustices. In the past, Florida State has had a mass camp-out on Landis Green that lasted over a month.

Minority Clubs on Campus

There are quite a few organizations on campus that represent minorities and offer them a voice in student affairs. The list of organizations includes the African Student Association, the Chinese Student & Scholar Association, the Cuban American Student Association, and the South Asian Students Association.

Students Speak Out On...
Diversity

Q Very Diverse Campus
There are quite a few races and ethnicities on campus and everyone is very welcoming and open to other people's backgrounds and beliefs.

Q All Are Welcome
There are over 500 student run organizations on Florida State's campus, all of which are diverse. Everybody will be able to find where they fit in the most. There is no excuse not to get involved because if you don't like any of the 500 organizations, you are more than welcome to start your own. It is actually encouraged.

Q Lots of Diversity
There are so many different types of races and religions at FSU and the great thing about it is that everyone is accepted. There are the typical greek sororities and fraternities but then you also have an array of multicultural fraternities and sororities as well. There are also tons of clubs and organizations for differences in political beliefs, religion, and sexual orientation.

Q Diversity!
Diversity on campus is great! There are so many different types of people, and that alone teaches new and old students to engage in meeting new friends of all types. Many events are organized by many different types of people, leading to a successful and interesting event. Also there are many groups and organizations dedicated to the acceptance of all races throughout the college community.

From being an Bisexual Asian girl to an Islamic American, there will definitely always be a place for you to mingle and make friends!

Q Diversity Central

In my opinion there is diversity at FSU, and alot of it. My roommate was Jamaican and she had a friend who was Haitian. She introduced me to a culture that I had never experienced and wouldn't have been able to if it hadn't been for her.

Q Very Open to Diversity

The school has a wide array of diversity. There are clubs and organizations for different races, political beliefs, religion, sexual orientation, you name it! Most people that I have come across have been very accpeting to everyones's different beliefs and ideals.

Q So Many Different Races

There is a bunch of different ethnicitys around campus. Probabably more white than anything but there is still plenty of different races

Q Diversity Amid Population

Diversity at Florida State is pretty apparent. Over half of the student body is female with races ranging from all corners of the world. There is also a great feeling of acceptance in clubs, organizations and societies.

The College Prowler Take On...
Diversity

Florida State appears to strive towards diversity among the student body. Recent statistics show that FSU has seen minority enrollment increase over 30 percent in the last few years. In addition to financial assistance and aid programs for the economically challenged, the school also offers the CARE program to assist students in adjusting to the social and academic atmosphere. FSU also boasts a large number of international students, as well as over 250 student organizations. This broad range of representation will give students the opportunity to meet and hang out with people of a similar background and to intermingle with people from different backgrounds. Also, keep in mind that Florida A&M University, a predominately minority school, is only a few blocks away, which serves to deepen the ethnic and cultural diversity of the area. Most students agree that attending FSU is a great way to broaden your horizons and gain exposure to a variety of people and cultures.

Even though it is firmly situated in a conservative, government-oriented town, FSU has a diversity that is competitive with any institute of higher learning. Florida State is a model ethnic melting pot, with the student body being comprised of a large number of African Americans, Asian Americans, and Hispanic Americans. The school also has a number of ethnic-based student associations that offer a wide range of services and support. FSU is also open-minded enough to include a gay, bisexual, and transgendered student organization that not only offers camaraderie in a group setting, but also support for those in need and a proud and outspoken proponent on campus issues.

The College Prowler® Grade on

Diversity: B

A high grade in Diversity indicates that ethnic minorities and international students have a notable presence on campus and that students of different economic backgrounds, religious beliefs, and sexual preferences are well-represented.

Guys & Girls

The Lowdown On...
Guys & Girls

Female Undergrads
55%

Male Undergrads
45%

Birth Control Available?

Yes: At Thagard Student Health Center

Social Scene

The majority of students will agree that Florida State is one of the friendliest places in the country. Sure, it can be awkward at first, but it won't take long to meet new people and find a crowd to hang out with.

Hookups or Relationships?

While there are a number of couples on campus, there is also a thriving singles scene. There are several bars on the edge of campus—along the Tennessee Street Strip—that cater to the singles crowd with ladies-night drink specials and other events that offer the opportunity to mix and mingle.

Dress Code

The students at FSU tend to dress casually. There are a few who are brave enough to dress up, but you have to remember, this is Florida, and the summer here can be warm and humid. From May to October, most people will be wearing shorts, T-shirts, and flip-flops. This isn't to say that they dress like slobs—just that most students dress for comfort.

Did You Know?

Top Five Places to Hook Up:
1. Doak Campbell Stadium
2. Landis Green
3. Strozier Library
4. Off-campus parties
5. The Capitol Building

Top Places to Find Hotties:
1. FSU Reservation at Lake Bradford
2. Leach Athletic Center
3. The Tennessee Street Strip

Students Speak Out On...
Guys & Girls

Q **Ready to Have a Good Time**

Tallahassee is a party city for college students, but at the same time there are many resources available to help these party animals pass their classes. There are a huge variety of students and even within Greek life the personality of each sorority /fraternity is unbelievably different.

Q **Lots of Girls**

There are so many girls at the school that males are the minority almost it seems. Thats enough said.

Q **Flrorida State University**

The guys and girls at Florida State are both pretty amazing. There are some stuck up women and some very douche baggy guys but for the most part everyone is really down to earth and willing to help anyone else out. The good thing about the intresets students have is that they're all sooo different. There huge variety in every program so a new freshman will sure be able to find their niche. Greek life is huge a Florida State there are a lot of sorority and fraternity guys and gals but you get used to it quickly.

Q **Best of Both Worlds**

The guys are smart, into sports, and big on seminole pride. The girls, well... we did win best looking student body in the country

Q **Girls Are Everywhere**

At Florida State expect to see plenty of attractive women around anytime you are on campus. There is plenty of diversity and you really can find anyone that fits what you look for in a woman.

Q Girls Are HOT!

First time I walked on the Florida State Campus as a high school senior, I thought I was on a model shoot. Everywhere you walk there are beautiful women. The best part of the year is obviously sorority rush when you see all the beautiful girls walking around in their best dress. If you go out to the strip or any of the clubs you can find a very large collection of drop dead gorgeous women

Q Social Life

At FSU, its very hard not to have a social life. There is something going on every night. If you don't go out one night, you're not missing out on much, because sure enough something else is going on the next night. Going out and partying is a great way to socialize and meet new people.

Q Community College

Many different people attend school here. You would see the same people in the grocery store or anywhere else.

The College Prowler Take On...
Guys & Girls

Most students at FSU will admit that one of the more popular pastimes on campus is admiring the student body. The warm weather offers ample opportunity to bask in the sun. It also gives people a chance to show a little more skin. It can sometimes be distracting during the summer months, but you'd be hard-pressed to find someone that complains about it. As if that weren't enough, FSU students are also some of the friendliest in the South. Of course, in Tallahassee, the women outnumber men at a little over two to one, but that doesn't interfere with anyone making new friends.

Both the male and female students here are not afraid to show their stuff, especially during the warmer months. One of the more popular activities on campus is sitting on Landis Green and admiring other students basking in the warm summer sun. You can also attend the regularly-scheduled bikini and hard body contests sponsored by some of the local drinking establishments. Besides being easy on the eyes, the student body here also tends to be friendly and sociable. People aren't afraid to say hello or offer assistance if you look like you're in need. Southern hospitality is contagious, and FSU is considered one of the most student-friendly campuses in the nation.

A

**The College Prowler®
Grade on**

Guys & Girls

A high grade for Guys or Girls indicates that the students on campus is attractive, smart, friendly, and engaging, and that the school has a decent gender ratio.

A+

Guys: A

Girls: A+

Athletics

The Lowdown On...
Athletics

Athletic Association
NAA
NCAA

Athletic Division
NCAA Division I-A

Athletic Conferences
Football: Atlantic Coast
Conference
Basketball: Atlantic Coast
Conference

School Colors
Garnet and gold

**School Nickname/
Mascot**
Seminole Indian

**Men Playing Varsity
Sports**
334: 3%

Women Playing Varsity Sports
292: 2%

Men's Varsity Sports
Baseball
Basketball
Football
Golf
Swimming and diving
Tennis
Track and field

Women's Varsity Sports
Basketball
Golf
Soccer
Softball
Swimming and diving
Tennis
Track and field
Volleyball

Intramurals
Basketball
Bowling
Flag football
Home run derby
Kickball
Racquetball
Soccer
Softball
Swimming
Table tennis
Tailgate games
Tennis
Ultimate Frisbee

Volleyball
Wallyball
Weightlifting
Wiffleball

Club Sports
Aikido
Badminton
Baseball
Bowling
Climbing
Crew
Cricket
Cuong Nhu
Cycling
Equestrian
Fencing
Field hockey
Gymnastics
Ice hockey
Kiteboarding
Lacrosse (men's and women's)
Paintball
Racquetball
Roller hockey
Rugby (men's and women's)
Scuba
Shotokan Karate
Skimming
Soccer (men's and women's)
Softball
Surfing
Swimming
Table tennis
Tennis
Triathlon
Ultimate Frisbee
Volleyball (men's and women's)
Wakeboarding

Water polo (men's and
women's)
Wrestling

Students Receiving Athletic Financial Aid

Football: 92
Basketball: 24
Baseball: 32
Cross Country/Track: 63
Other Sports: 135

Graduation Rates of Athletic Financial Aid Recipients

Football: 79%
Basketball: 75%
Baseball: 38%
Cross Country/Track: 36%
Other Sports: 69%

Athletic Fields & Facilities

Leach Recreation Center
Scott Speicher Tennis Center
Seminole Golf Course
Stults Aquatic Center
Tully Gym

Most Popular Sports
Baseball, football, softball, volleyball

Most Overlooked Teams
Women's basketball, women's soccer, lacrosse

School Spirit
School spirit is taken to the extreme at Florida State, especially during football season. The homecoming parade actually shuts down part of downtown Tallahassee. Game days are completely nuts. Be prepared to see nothing but garnet and gold everywhere you look. This is especially true when in-state rivals University of Florida or the University of Miami come to town. FSU students take great pride in their school, and it shows.

Getting Tickets
It is very easy to get tickets to most sporting events at FSU. All currently enrolled students pay an athletics fee with their tuition, so student tickets are free. For large events like football games, students request their tickets online, and block seating is available. A lottery will be used when student demand for tickets exceed the supply of available tickets, but usually this doesn't happen. For other events, students show their FSU ID to the ticket office located near Doak Campbell Stadium to receive their free ticket to the game.

Best Place to Take a Walk
San Luis Mission Park, St. Mark's Trail

Did You Know?

In the wake of the NCAA's 2005 decision not to support most Native American-themed mascots, there arose some uncertainty as to whether FSU could retain its use of the name "Seminoles," as well as images and symbols representing that name. A council meeting of the Seminole Tribe's elders in June of 2005, however, affirmed that the Tribe's relationship with FSU was a constructive one, and that FSU's traditions and depiction of the Seminole were respectful.

Students Speak Out On...
Athletics

Q Athletics

Florida State University is a very school spirited unviversities with multiple national titles. They have great recruiting and have almost any sport someone would be looking for. Our big sports are football and baseball. On gamedays we have ESPN trailing us on the field and the crowds are usually a sellout. Our IM's are also very good and competitive yet fun. We also have a few club leagues for people not on the college "varsity" level yet they are more competitive than at the IM level.

Q Noles Hit Goals!

I'm not too familiar with sports, but the noles are great! I just moved to this little, yet fun-filled college city and although it's a nice change and am enjoying it here, I'm also struggling to get by! I really hope this scholarship comes through for me!!

Q Stereotypical Southern School

Football is the core of FSU in many ways. During the fall, you will run into classmates, friends, and professors on their way to the stadium to watch the home game. When it's not football season, basketball and baseball both get a fair amount of attention. There are also intramural sports throughout the year for any student at every skill level.

Q Let's Go Noles!

Sports are actually a big part of life as a Seminole. Football games are the most popular in the fall, but no sports are overlooked. They are all supported by a very spirited fan base and all are popular to participate as well as to watch. The facilities are all phenomenal. We have the nicest baseball stadium I've seen at a big state school. Our Doak Campbell Stadium is gorgeous and very functional, and usually full. It is incredible to see more than half the stadium partake in the Tomahawk Chop and rooting for our teams!

Q The Noles Are FEIRCE.

Sports at FSU are always a big deal. This goes for varsity and IM. The students are very supportive and it's always a good time.

Q FSU Football Is Fantastic

Although Florida State excels in many of the sports that it participates, the experience of being at a football game is unbeatable. The pride and spirit that fans, alumni, and students have for their Seminoles makes everyone who attends want to shout with the war-chant and cheer on our excellent team.

Q Amazing!

Our fanbase is huge! So many seminole fans! Lots of team spirit!

Q Sports Are a Part of FSU Life

Football is huge, especially this coming season with a new coach and a tough schedule. The whole school shuts down on home game days. Our other sports get a lot of student support also. Our school has a great reputation in sports. Fans and students love to come out for the atmosphere of it all. The facilities are top notch. FSU uses students in the right areas to help athletes with fitness, nutrition, tutoring, all sorts of stuff. It is a great way to keep everyone involved, not just athletes.

The College Prowler Take On...
Athletics

For those who want to participate in sports but aren't ready to try out at the varsity level, it's easy to get involved with intramural teams. There is a wide variety of IMs to choose from, and the warm weather allows for year-round competition. IM sports are plentiful and offer a variety of choices for the discerning amateur athlete. The choices run the gamut, from flag football to bowling. All the IM sports are well organized and highly competitive, so make sure you're serious about the sport you choose, otherwise you may end up on the sidelines.

As for varsity sports at FSU, football is arguably the biggest thing on campus. When fall rolls around, you can feel the excitement in the air. Tickets can be difficult to come by, especially for the big games, but everyone is usually able to attend the games they want. Florida State University prides itself on having one of the most competitive athletic programs in the country. Football dominates the scene, but that doesn't mean the other sports are ignored. FSU women's sports are just as competitive as the men's and also garner national attention, with the softball, soccer, and volleyball teams often in the hunt for a national championship. Even if you aren't interested in sports, you can't help but cheer when an FSU team takes the field.

A-

The College Prowler® Grade on

Athletics: A

A high grade in Athletics indicates that students have school spirit, that sports programs are respected, that games are well-attended, and that intramurals are a prominent part of student life.

Nightlife

The Lowdown On...
Nightlife

Cheapest Place to Get a Drink
Bullwinkle's

Primary Areas with Nightlife
Downtown
Gaines Street
Railroad Avenue
Tennessee Street Strip

Closing Time
2 a.m.

Useful Resources for Nightlife
www.tallahassee.com/mld/tallahassee/entertainment
www.tallystudents.com

Club Listings
Potbelly's
459 W. College Ave.
Tallahassee
(850) 224-2233
www.potbellys.net
Description: This is one of
the most popular hangouts in
Tallahassee, with a bar, dance
floor, and outside patio if you
want to get away from the
noise. However, don't get
caught there on a weekend;
this is the place to go on
Tuesdays and Thursdays.

Bar Listings
Beta Bar
809 Railroad Ave.
Tallahassee
(850) 425-2697
www.thebetabar.com
This is arguably one of the
best places in town to catch
live music from both local
and national bands. Live
music is offered throughout
the week, giving you the
chance to hear everything
from reggae to hardcore
punk. The Beta Bar also has
pinball, pool, and foosball.

Brothers
926 W. Tharpe St.
Tallahassee
(850) 386-2399
Brothers is said to be one
of the funkiest nightclubs

in town. They offer
entertainment ranging from
drag shows to Old Wave
parties. Definitely not to be
missed.

Bullwinkle's
620 W. Tennessee St.
Tallahassee
(850) 224-0651
www.bullwinklessaloon.net
Ranked by Playboy magazine
as one of the best college
bars in the country, it features
an indoor dance club, live
music in the Jamaican Beer
Garden, and offers a Thirsty
Moose VIP Club.

Club Downunder
FSU Student Union
On campus
(850)644-6710
union.fsu.edu/cdu
This is an on-campus
nightspot that offers live
music and comedy, as well
other various performance
opportunities throughout the
week.

Floyd's Music Store
666 W. Tennessee St.
Tallahassee
(850) 222-3506
www.floydsmusicstore.com
Another hot place to catch
live music on the weekend,
Floyd's also offers a variety
of drink specials and
18-and-over shows.

Gordo's
1907 W. Pensacola St.
Tallahassee
(850) 576-5767
www.gordoscubanfood.com
Cuban restaurant by day and student hangout by night, Gordo's is one of the cheaper places in Tallahassee to get a drink. Friday is Latin night, and Thursdays feature cheap pitchers all day long.

The Grove
111 W. College Ave.
Tallahassee
(850) 577-0700
The Grove is small, but it's still very popular. The dress code is fairly strict—it's more of a Miami kind of lounge than Tallahassee's other nightspots.

Late Night Library
809 Gay St.
Tallahassee
(850) 224-2429
One of Tallahassee's more unique spots, the Library is divided into three rooms—two of which are outside—and concentrates much more on music and dancing than most other local bars.

The Moon
1105 E. Lafayette St.
Tallahassee
(850) 878.6900

www.moonevents.com
Wednesdays are college nights at the Moon, a bar and music venue which adopts a completely different vibe for each night of the week.

Po'Boys Creole Café
1944 W. Pensacola St.
Tallahassee
(850) 574-4144
www.poboys.com
As the name implies, Po'Boys specializes in Creole food and exhibits a lively Baton Rouge atmosphere. Great jambalaya, authentic gumbo, and a free-beer-for-ladies Tuesday make this place a popular hangout for FSU students.

Other Places to Check Out

4th Quarter Bar & Grille
A.J.'s Sports Bar
Café Cabernet
Calico Jack's Seafood House & Oyster Bar
Club Jade
Down Below
Ken's
Leon Pub
Paradise Grill & Bar
Poor Paul's Pourhouse
Posy's
Potbelly's
Snooker's
Stetson's
Waterworks

Favorite Drinking Games

Card games
Century Club
Power Hour
Quarters

What to Do if You're Not 21

You can get in to some bars, like Floyd's, Late Night Library, and the Beta Bar. They often have 18-and-over nights

Organization Parties

The organizations and clubs on campus are always active and ready for a good time. In addition to regular events, some hold private or invitation-only parties. They may not always be as big or as loud as some of the Greek parties, but they are always fun.

Students Speak Out On...
Nightlife

Q Perfect "College Experience."

College is not all about partying and being a social butterfly; But when it comes to FSU, this school has every other one beat as far as night life goes. Every party is a total blow out- Numerous kegs, beerpong tables, and usually even a little liquor bar set up. Bars and clubs are always very accomodating to girls. They usually allow us to pay a cheaper cover fee than guys.(which is fine with me!) Every night of the week there is some bar or club that is open and popular for that specific night of the week. College students here know where to frequent! Plus, after a long night of drinking, there are numerous "safe buses" to transport you safely home!

Q Nightlife

The nightlife here at FSU is awesome. Many different clubs to go to if you're 18 or older.

Q Nightlife at FSU

The nightlife is probably one of the best of any college. Tallahassee is a college town so you don't have to be 21 to get into a club/bar most are 18-and-up. There are many different types of places you can go- whether you want to just shoot some pool, play darts and drink a beer or if you want to get dressed up and go clubbing for the night. Mostly everything is open until 2-3am and there is a public bus called "The Night Nole" that is free and will take you all around Tallahassee to the major student apartment complexes so you don't drink and drive. You can also always call a taxi and you usually won't spend more than $10. The bars and clubs are within walking distance from campus so if you live on campus most people just walk. But if that doesn't sound like your thing, there are always house parties that hire DJ's.

Q AWESOME!!!!

I love Florida State University! It has great nightlife atmosphere! There are always parties going on and the clubs are awesome. I love Tallahassee! Though to some people it seems dangerous because it is the capitol, but once you live there for a while it all grows on you and you can't help but go out at night and LIVE IT UP!

Q Awesome Night Life

The bars are great and cheap and the deals are sweet. House parties are also everywhere and are a great time.

Q Tallahassee Nightlife!

Tallahassee is the place to be! There are parties every week, from nightclub parties to Greek sponsored events. Most all events also offer free transportation, like shuttles, and Florida State has the "Night Nole" bus, which runs extra late, and for free, for the party-goers. You'll also meet party-people from the other two colleges: Florida A&M and Tallahassee Community. Clubs are 18+, and drinking is a big part of the Tallahassee party scene.

Q Something to Do Every Night

There is something going on every night at FSU! Most of the clubs are 18-and-older so no one has a problem getting in, house parties are a common occurrence as well. The bus system here runs until 3:00 a.m. so getting home is never an issue.

Q Always Something to Do!

There are always house parties, always something cool at the clubs, the people are always ready to have fun, and always lots of fun.

The College Prowler Take On...
Nightlife

New arrivals to Florida State may be fooled into thinking that Tallahassee is a sleepy, Southern town, but the truth of the matter is that the nightlife here is alive and well. On any given night, you can have your choice of live music, dancing, and drink specials. The Greeks on campus have a reputation of throwing some of the best bashes, and the off-campus parties often wind up being large and loud. Most students will hang out on the Tennessee Street Strip, but bars and clubs surround the campus. Remember that this is a two-college town, so there are going to be some crazy parties to attend almost every weekend, whether they are FSU parties or not, and whether they on campus or off.

However, all this partying does bring some unwanted attention. The local police department recently established a "Party Patrol" that responds to complaints about off-campus parties and underage drinking, and the FSU police are fairly strict, as well. Because the students at FSU are so friendly and outgoing, you won't have to worry about being bored. There's always a good time to be found around every corner, just use common sense to stay safe and to not get caught.

A

The College Prowler® Grade on
Nightlife: A

A high grade in Nightlife indicates that there are many bars and clubs in the area that are easily accessible and affordable. Other determining factors include the number of options for the under-21 crowd and the prevalence of house parties.

Greek Life

The Lowdown On...
Greek Life

Undergrad Men in Fraternities
14%

Number of Sororities
26

Undergrad Women in Sororities
14%

Number of Fraternities
32

Fraternities

Alpha Delta Phi
Alpha Epsilon Pi
Alpha Phi Alpha
Alpha Tau Omega
Chi Phi
Delta Chi
Delta Tau Delta
Iota Phi Theta
Kappa Alpha
Kappa Alpha Psi
Kappa Sigma
Lambda Chi Alpha
Lambda Theta Phi
Omega Psi Phi
Phi Beta Sigma
Phi Delta Theta
Phi Gamma Delta
Phi Iota Alpha
Phi Kappa Psi
Phi Kappa Tau
Phi Sigma Kappa
Pi Kappa Alpha
Pi Kappa Phi
Pi Lambda Phi
Sigma Alpha Epsilon
Sigma Beta Rho
Sigma Chi
Sigma Lambda Beta
Sigma Nu
Sigma Pi
Tau Kappa Epsilon
Theta Chi

Sororities

Alpha Chi Omega
Alpha Delta Pi
Alpha Gamma Delta
Alpha Kappa Alpha
alpha Kappa Delta Phi

Chi Omega
Delta Delta Delta
Delta Gamma
Delta Sigma Theta
Delta Zeta
Gamma Phi Beta
Kappa Alpha Theta
Kappa Delta
Kappa Delta Chi
Kappa Kappa Gamma
Lambda Tau Omega
Lambda Theta Alpha
Phi Mu
Pi Beta Phi
Sigma Delta Tau
Sigma Gamma Rho
Sigma Iota Alpha
Sigma Lambda Gamma
Theta Nu Xi
Zeta Phi Beta
Zeta Tau Alpha

Multicultural Colonies

Alpha Kappa Alpha (NPHC)
alpha Kappa Delta Phi (MGC)
Alpha Phi Alpha (NPHC)
Delta Sigma Theta (NPHC)
Iota Phi Theta (NPHC)
Kappa Alpha Psi (NPHC)
Kappa Delta Chi (MGC)
Lambda Tau Omega (MGC)
Lambda Theta Alpha (MGC)
Lambda Theta Phi (MGC)
Omega Psi Phi (NPHC)
Phi Beta Sigma (NPHC)
Phi Iota Alpha (MGC)
Sigma Beta Rho (MGC)
Sigma Gamma Rho (NPHC)
Sigma Iota Alpha (MGC)
Sigma Lambda Beta (MGC)

Sigma Lambda Gamma (MGC)
Theta Nu Xi (MGC)
Zeta Phi Beta (NPHC)

Other Greek Organizations

Interfraternity Council
Multicultural Greek Council
National Pan-Hellenic Council
Order of Omega
Panhellenic Association

Students Speak Out On...
Greek Life

Q Haven't Noticed Yet...
I haven't really payed attention to the Greek life here at FSU, but I'm sure it's great for all those who are a part of it (with the variety and closeness of all students) here!

Q Greek Life
Greek life is a big part of campus. A good majority of the students participate in some kind of Greek life events. There are also lots of options to choose from.

Q Greeks Are Pretty Dominate
Greek Life is pretty dominate at FSU, but they don't "reign supreme" or anything.If you're not in one, it's not a big issue. Greeks at Florida State have "Sorority Row," basically, streets of sorority and frat houses! Also, ethnic (Black,Hispanic,& Multicultural) Greeks play a big role in campus life and social events. Ethnic Greek groups provide numerous forms of fun weekly entertainment, including stepping/dancing, and hosting events and parties.

Q Greek Life at FSU
We have beautifully maintained houses and a nice party scene.

Q I <3 Greek Life
Greek life is awesome. Everyone should join FSU's greek system. If not, you're not cool.

Q Greek Life Rules
I personally am a "Greek" myself and a proud sister of the new sorority Alpha Phi at Florida State. Although we do

not have a permanent house as of yet, our sorority remains extremely close and active in the Greek community. Every sorority and fraternity has been very welcoming to Alpha Phi. Greek life heavily participates in almost all student based activities as well as with the entire community. Many non-Greeks view Greeks in a negative manner, but usually after hanging out with them change their minds. One doesn't have to be Greek to fit into the school; however, being active in the Greek community makes the college experience much more fun.

Q Greek Life

Greek Life at FSU provides coutless opportunities to do community service and meet new people. Everyone is excited to help out around the community. I believe Greeks and Non-greeks get allong very well! Also, the housing is great heritage grove is a community of frat houses and its perfect for attending parties.

Q I Love It

Joining the greek life at my school was the best decision I made. I joined as a sophomore and can definetely say it has made me appreciate my school way more. Whenever the school is hosting an event of any sort the first organization they turn to is Greek life. Therefore, you know everything that is going on in school and have a foot in the door in basically anything you want to join. I love it!

The College Prowler Take On...
Greek Life

Like any major university, FSU has an active and thriving Greek scene. Rush week is always a huge event, with an almost endless succession of parties and gatherings that allow potential members the opportunity to learn all there is about the fraternity or sorority they are most interested in. However, Greek organizations tend to have a partying reputation, but many students do not notice all of the volunteer work the Greeks perform—all of the time and effort that goes into these events. For example, the Greek community at FSU has raised and donated over $100,000 and 20,000 service hours to charitable organizations over the past academic year. Despite many of the preconceptions, Greek organizations at FSU set the standard for leadership and community service.

As far as the social scene is concerned, Greek life is not "the" dominant force on campus. Some students enjoy the camaraderie and lifelong friendships they develop through membership in a fraternity or sorority. Greeks throw parties, but so do other organizations. The Greeks do dominate student government and homecoming elections, but that is to be expected, and that is how it is at any major university. The majority of students at FSU do not belong to a fraternity or sorority, and many would agree that their social lives are just as active as any Greek's.

The College Prowler® Grade on
Greek Life: A-

A high grade in Greek Life indicates that sororities and fraternities are not only present, but also active on campus. Other determining factors include the variety of houses available and the respect the Greek community receives from the rest of the campus.

www.collegeprowler.com

Drug Scene

The Lowdown On...
Drug Scene

Most Popular Drugs
Adderall
Alcohol
Marijuana

**Alcohol-Related
Referrals**
188

**Alcohol-Related
Arrests**
152

Drug-Related Referrals
3

Drug-Related Arrests
90

Drug Counseling Programs
University Counseling Center (UCC)
113 S. Wildwood Dr., Rm. 201
(850) 644-2003
Counseling, crisis intervention, referrals, workshops and
presentations

Students Speak Out On...
Drug Scene

Q There Is a Lot of Drinking...That's for Sure.

This is a party school. We have a lot of smart people and our share of not so smart people. Those are the ones who wander out on to Tennessee street and get hit. Other than that the alcohol/drug scene is not that bad.

Q Typical College Town

The Drug Scene is not that big, although you do hear of people smoking marijuana every now and then, but like any typical college town, drinking is the much more popular activity.

Q Florida State University

Drug use on FSU's campus is a very bad idea. FSU police is very good about cracking down and getting you into trouble. Alcohol use is very easy to do if you're smart and no obnoxious. If you're drinking in a dorm and being generally quiet and conserved about it, you'll be fine. But if you're drinking in your dorm with music BLASTING and you and your friends are screaming. Chances are, you're gonna get caught. My advice, find someone who lives off campus and do your illegal things there.

Q Drug-Free

everyone is always sober and not under-the-influence.

Q Drinking Is Popular

Every party I have been to has offered alcoholic drinks, but surprisingly no one has ever pressured me to drink anything.

Q Personal Responsibility to Self and FSU Is Expected

FSU although considered to many to be a "party school" has instilled in many the personal responsibility you have to yourself, others and FSU. There is a no tolerance for underage drinking, disorderly conduct, and drug use by the campus police. The majority of parties held on and off campus involve drinking while most do so responsibly, but there are a select few that have pushed the limit but ususally they do not get invited back to parties. There are many activities available that are drug and alcohol free. I feel that both men and women would feel comfortable at FSU and not presseured to partake in such activities.

Q Drinking Is More Popular

The only drugs on campus are really just smoking. Everything is more centered on drinking.

Q No Biggie

Weed is big around here, but hey, where isn't it. Party drugs are popular, as are drugs like ritalin and adderall for studying purposes. However, alcohol is far more popular and problematic than all the others combined.

The College Prowler Take On...
Drug Scene

While illegal drugs are present on campus, they aren't highly visible, and most students don't pay much attention to them. Alcohol and marijuana are the drugs of choice, although harder stuff, like ecstasy and amphetamines are available if you know where to look. Although some hard drugs are present, serious abuse is not a problem here. FSU does have a student chapter of NORML (National Organization for the Reform of Marijuana Laws), and we recently saw the first of what is planned to become an annual Hemp Fest held in Doak Campbell Stadium.

FSU has a very strict drug policy. However, the users and abusers tend to stay off the radar, so you won't hear much about arrests and expulsions. For the most part, the drug culture is quiet and secretive. People who want to be involved in it can find it on their own, while those who prefer to stay clean won't be tempted. Drugs aren't pushed on anyone, and no one will be forced to do them should they choose not to. It isn't as if dealers are vending their wares in the hallways.

The College Prowler® Grade on
Drug Scene: C

A high grade in the Drug Scene indicates that drugs are not a noticeable part of campus life; drug use is not visible, and no pressure to use them seems to exist.

Campus Strictness

The Lowdown On...
Campus Strictness

Students Are Most Likely to Get Caught...
Bringing food or drink in a cluster
Cheating
Downloading copyrighted materials
Drinking underage
Making too much noise in your dorm
Parking illegally
Running stop signs
Sending unsolicited e-mail (spam)
Skinny dipping in Westcott Fountain
Trespassing

Students Speak Out On...
Campus Strictness

Q Responsibility of Freedom

This school understands that you are of adult age or close when entering college and treat you as such. The motto they emphasize at orientation is "Responsibility of freedom." Pretty much it means we're not going to watch your every move, but if you mess up plagiarizing or you're caught on campus with drugs, the penalty is huge.

Q Easy Going

they are not very strict but, instead, quite informative and friendly.

Q Strictness

When it comes to underage drinking and drugs the campus police are pretty strict when it happen in the dorms. The outcome really depends on the situation. Normally warnings are given out. They are not too strict here

Q Strictness

The campus isn't that strict, they have their guidelines for what is expected and they are only enforced when challenged.

Q Not Very Strict at All

I can't recall any type of incident of my friends or myself getting into trouble so far... FSU is a well-known party school, so for the most part students do their thing. Your biggest look-out is really the TPD, they are EVERYWHERE.

Q They Mean What They Say

The campus police and the dorm security are very stict about the rules and school policies and do not hesitate to implement disciplinary action. The school takes this so serious that the The Florida State University Police shall be notified of all on campus events that are not regularly scheduled that plan to serve alcohol. These are the University State and Local Penalties. Possession or attempt to purchase alcohol by a person under 21 years of age, using a false driver's license ID or allowing someone to use your driver's license for an ID card and providing alcohol to a person under 21 has a typical first time offense resulting in Diversion program; $180 fine; 10 hours community work program with a maximum first time offense of 60 days jail; $500 fine. The biggest thing you can do to protect yourself from disciplinary action is to make sure you do not drink, try to obtain, or serve alcohol to any one under the age of 21.

Q Strictness

I think the campus is pretty lenient. Just don't do really stupid things and the school is fine.

Q Strict

The dorm RA's a very strict about alcohol in the dorms.

The College Prowler Take On...
Campus Strictness

Over the past several years, FSU has been trying to tone down the party-school reputation and put more emphasis on academics and athletics. Underage drinking is the biggest problem on campus, and the FSUPD are ever-vigilant when it comes to monitoring on-campus festivities. The quiet, subdued affairs generally don't have any problems. When things get loud is when the FSUPD steps in. This is not to say you still can't have a good time. On-campus parties are frequent, especially during football season. However, to avoid trouble with the school, it's best to party off campus. Just be aware of what you're doing, keep things under control, and party smart. Respect the police and they'll respect you.

Campus police don't play around when is comes to underage drinking. FSU has a strict policy about that, as well as drug use. Expulsion is not unheard of, and several Greek houses have been censured by the University. As long as things are kept under control, the campus cops won't break up the party. As soon as things begin to get rowdy, be prepared to see the blue flashing lights pull up outside. The main thing to watch out for is the Tallahassee Police Department. They have established a Party Patrol that not only roams the streets, but also responds to neighborhood complaints. These guys do not mess around. If they show up, expect them to write a ticket or two. If they don't show up, you have nothing to worry about. If you don't get too loud, you should be fine.

B-

The College Prowler® Grade on
Campus Strictness: B-

A high Campus Strictness grade implies an overall lenient atmosphere; police and RAs are fairly tolerant, and the administration's rules are flexible.

Parking

The Lowdown On...
Parking

Parking Services
FSU Parking &
Transportation
University Center Building
C-5406
(850) 644-5278
www.parking.fsu.edu

Approximate Parking
Permit Cost
Included in tuition as
Transportation Access Fee

Student Parking Lot
Yes: There are more than
20 parking lots and garages
on campus. About half of
these are commuter lots, and
the other half are open 24
hours for students living on
campus.

Freshmen Allowed to
Park
Yes

Common Parking Tickets

Expired meter: $20
Fire lane: $100
Handicapped zone: $250
No parking zone: $20

Getting a Parking Permit

All students pay a transportation fee with tuition and receive one free parking permit valid for the entire school year. Visitors can park for $3.25/day or $51.75/semester. Faculty and commercial vendors pay yearly fees for their parking permits.

Did You Know?

Best Places to Find a Parking Spot
There are no good lots. It's first come, first serve.
Arrive early if you expect to have a chance at
getting a spot.

Good Luck Getting a Parking Spot Here!
Just about anywhere on campus.

Students Speak Out On...
Parking

ℚ Parking Is Okay
Parking on campus can be a bit difficult if you are not acquainted with the campus. There are many lots where students can park, but they are not necessarily on campus (across the street). Permits are part of the tuition.

ℚ Parking
There are so many students and parking is a pain to find and you mostly have to find someone leaving in order to find a spot. If you get there early or really late you wont have much of a problem but in the afternoon its bad. There are lots located throughout the campus and permits are free.

ℚ Come an Hour Early!
Parking at FSU is the reason I live on campus. During peak class times, you can search for parking for up to an hour. I know plenty of people who purposely park somewhere illegal and just take the parking ticket because it's worth not dealing with the hassle of finding parking.

ℚ Parking Fail
Although a car can be helpful, it is hard to find a spot at FSU. You are better off walking or even...walking more.

ℚ Ugh Parking
parking is free but a bit of a hassle so I dont want to bring my car

Q Get There Early!

There are many parking spaces available, but few near the dorms or classrooms. To get a good parking spot, get there early. As soon as you move your car you will lose your spot. Also, DO NOT park in teacher parking. You will get towed and fined!

Q Horrible Parking

From all the stories and from what I've seen, parking at FSU is a monster. There are never any spots and the towing company are ready to pick up any car at a moments notice. A car is not recommend for FSU unless you live far from campus.

Q Average Parking Situation

Parking at FSU is not the greatest, but there is really no need for a car on campus. We have one of the best public transportation systems for students. But if buses aren't your thing, you can literally walk anywhere on campus within 15 minutes. If you do decide to drive, commuter lots are usually best.

The College Prowler Take On...
Parking

If you want to see an FSU student get all worked up, ask them about parking on campus. Most of the lots are full by 8:30 in the morning, and trying to get a spot after that is like looking for ice cubes in the desert. The general rule for students taking classes later in the day is to arrive at least 30 to 40 minutes ahead of time, and then be prepared to wait. FSU has taken small steps to improve the situation, but so far it hasn't been enough. Some students opt to ride bicycles, motorcycles, or scooters. They also rely on the local bus system. The school is serious about parking violations, and the tickets can be expensive. Also, unpaid fines will result not only in late fees, but also in holds being put on registration and graduation. Despite all the complaints, the school continues to drag its feet on fixing the problem.

The thing that gets most students angry is the fact that they have to pay a parking fee, but it doesn't guarantee a parking space. Most people end up circling the lots like vultures, waiting for someone to pull out so they can all scramble to fill the vacancy. The University doesn't allot spaces; it's a first-come, first-serve basis.

The College Prowler® Grade on
Parking: B-

A high grade in the Parking section indicates that parking is both available and affordable, and that parking enforcement isn't overly severe.

Transportation

The Lowdown On...
Transportation

Best Ways to Get Around Town

Bum a ride.

Ride a bike. Tallahassee has numerous bike lanes and trails.

Take the city bus because it's free with your student ID.

Walk, as long as it's close to campus. Tallahassee is very hilly.

Campus Shuttle
Seminole Express Bus
parking.fsu.edu/
transportation.html
7 a.m. to 7 p.m.

Public Transit
StarMetro
www.talgov.com/starmetro
Allows students with valid FSU IDs to ride without charge on all city bus routes on regular class days.

Best Ways to Get to the Airport

Alternatively, you can just take a cab; a cab ride to the airport costs approximately $20.

Capital Transportation (850) 580-8080

Croom's Transportation (850) 653-2466

Nearest Airport

Tallahassee Regional Airport

(850) 891-7802

The airport is approximately 6 miles southwest of campus.

Nearest Passenger Bus

Greyhound

112 W. Tennessee St.

(850) 222-4249 or (800) 231-2222

www.greyhound.com

The Greyhound terminal is located approximately four blocks from campus, across the street from the city bus terminal.

Students Speak Out On...
Transportation

ℚ Save on Gas and Time
Transportation at FSU is amazing. There are multiple bus routes that run all around town. They service those who live on campus as well as off. The buses are free for all students and usually run on time. At night, there is a longer bus route that services the same areas and runs all night. This is great in preventing drunk driving. Also, they offer the "Safe Bus" service. You can call their phone number or place a call through one of the emergency poles. The safe buses can drop you off anywhere on campus if you feel unsafe.

ℚ Buss Is Awesome
the bus can take you around campus in a very short amount of time, with the campus route coming every 10 mins and then other buses also circling school, you should never be late to class or not have transportation.

ℚ Very Effective
Have the campus buses that run every 15 mins, the city buses are free for FSU students with a college id

ℚ Very Easy to Get Around
Parking is very rarely a problem, & if you don't want to drive you can catch a free bus to pretty much any place you need to go.

ℚ Excellent
Taxis are cheap, especially since everything is within a five mile radius. On-campus bus is normally on time and free to students since it is included in our tuition. Public buses are also free to students, all you need to do is show your college ID

◯ Many Options

If you don't have a car, it's not that big of a deal. Tons of people ride bikes, skateboards, etc around campus and there's even a special "recycling" program at FSU where for $20 a you can rent a bike for a whole year. Also, we have a bus system that is free for everyone that goes around campus all day long and stops at the important places (the stadium, the gym, the Union, etc). The campus is not that big once you get used to it, so it may be easier to just walk. Our buses also go off campus near the popular apartment complexes, also for free. In addition, the Tallahassee Bus System is free for students if you show your student ID and it goes to Pubix, the Governor's Square Mall, CVS, and tons of restaurants. For long-distance trips, there are bus companies that take students to the major cities in Florida, such as Jacksonville, Tampa, Orlando, and Miami that cost around $75-$100 depending on the company.

◯ Seminole Express Is the Way to Go!

Florida State provides free transportation via bus around campus-stopping at nearby apartment complexes. It saves gas and money! It runs from early morning to extremely late at night.

◯ Convenience

The bus system is phenomenal. They are general good with being on time, and if not it's usually only by a few minutes, and they'll get you anywhere on campus- and even some off campus places. If the school buses wont get you there, then the city buses probably will. There are many accessible ways to get around here!

The College Prowler Take On...
Transportation

The FSU Seminole Express bus system is a reliable and safe way to get around campus, with service running on average of every 10–15 minutes. It's also free, which makes it extremely popular with the student body. StarMetro, Tallahassee's bus system, also offers free service with a valid student ID. Tallahassee can boast one of the better public transportation systems in the state. City buses are always a reliable way to get around town, and FSU has a regular bus route around campus that is a lifesaver during the heat of summer. There is also a downtown trolley that runs Monday through Friday, and taxis are always an option for those with money burning a hole in their pocket. In a pinch, you can always call a cab to get you around downtown or to one of the shopping malls.

If you're looking to venture outside the city limits, there are a number of car rental agencies close to campus. The Tallahassee Regional Airport also provides reliable service, but expect to pay more for airfare. Some people forego the local airport, renting a car, instead, and driving to Jacksonville or Atlanta to save a couple hundred dollars. Basically, as long as you aren't going too far, transportation around campus and the city is convenient and cheap.

The College Prowler® Grade on

Transportation: A-

A high grade for Transportation indicates that campus buses, public buses, cabs, and rental cars are readily-available and affordable. Other determining factors include proximity to an airport and the necessity of transportation.

Weather

The Lowdown On...
Weather

Temperature Averages
Spring – High: 80 °F
Spring – Low: 54 °F
Summer – High: 92 °F
Summer – Low: 72 °F
Fall – High: 81 °F
Fall – Low: 58 °F
Winter – High: 66 °F
Winter – Low: 41 °F

Precipitation Averages
Spring: 5.00 in.
Summer: 7.33 in.
Fall: 4.04 in.
Winter: 4.70 in.

Students Speak Out On...
Weather

ᗡ Mostly Perfect

I love the weather here because its mostly sunny besides the occasional thunder storms during hurricane season, but the winter is cold but not freezing and springtime is my favorite here.

ᗡ The Perfect Weather

Personally I'm from New York City, and the weather in Tallahassee is just perfect. It is cool (60-70) for the majority of the year, and in the winter it only drops down to the forties at the most. The summer is nice and warm and there are always people out tanning when the sun is out.

ᗡ Normally Wonderful!!!

FSU is located in Sunny Florida, so the weather is normally not a problem! However, this winter the campus got down to a chilly 19 degrees with a windchill factor making it 9 degrees!!!!! Bu the rest of the year is beautiful! Beware it does rain EVERY day in the Summer, but they are usually short and mild sperts.

ᗡ Very Nice

During the spring and beginning of Fall semesters the weather is beautiful, there is rarely a drop of rain and the sky is always clear.

ᗡ Weather

During the summer, it rains almost everyday. That is really annoying when you need to get to class, and teachers don't ever cancel class for rain. This winter was freezing cold, which is not something that any Floridian is used to, so that made it really hard to get up and go to class as well. But most of the time it is hot and sunny, and very enjoyable!

Q Not Used to Winter

I am from Orlando so I am not used to the winter being as cold as it was this year in Tallahassee. However, it did push me to stay in and study more, and other than the colder winters, the weather is generally the same as Orlando.

Q It's Florida

What can I say, it's Florida. We don't really have winter here and when the weather starts to turn to the warmer side, the fur boots are ditched for bikinis and sandals.

Q Lots of Rain, but No Snow!

It rains alot in Tallahassee, often without any warning. When it rains alot, areas of the campus can flood. Rain boots are a must in rainy weather when walking to class. Classes are sometime cancelled when the campus floods, or the rain is really heavy, but don't bank on it. It gets cold, you'll need a winter coat, but the fall and spring is great!

The College Prowler Take On...
Weather

Florida is called the Sunshine State for a reason. Even in the winter, the temperatures have been know to get as high as 70°F, and the coldest low on record is 2 below zero, but that hasn't occurred since 1899. The general opinion around campus is that, on average, the weather is great. The dead of summer can get extremely hot and humid, so when considering on living arrangements, make sure the place has a working air conditioner. The locals will grudgingly admit that winters here aren't too bad. Heavy coats aren't needed, except in rare occasions. Most students can get by with a couple of sweaters.

Weather in Tallahassee is usually predictable, which makes it easy to prepare before you come to school. Spring and fall are the best times of year because the temperatures are bearable. Summer can be nice, but the warmer temperatures can take some getting used to. It does have its advantages, however, like more time to spend at the beach or the FSU Reservation soaking up rays and admiring the local fauna. On the down side, all this beautiful weather can make it difficult to stay indoors studying. Sometimes, you have to make tough decisions.

The College Prowler® Grade on
Weather: B

A high Weather grade designates that temperatures are mild and rarely reach extremes, that the campus tends to be sunny rather than rainy, and that weather is fairly consistent rather than unpredictable.

www.collegeprowler.com

FLORIDA STATE UNIVERSITY
Report Card Summary

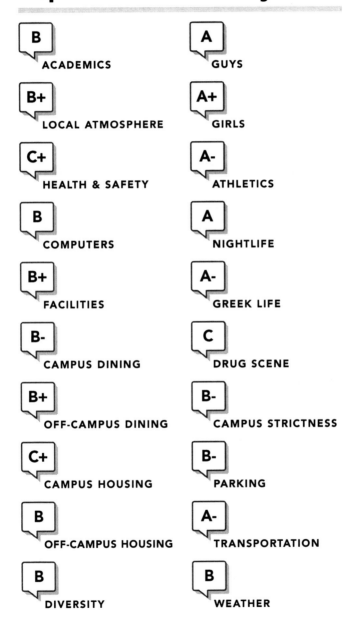

B
ACADEMICS

A
GUYS

B+
LOCAL ATMOSPHERE

A+
GIRLS

C+
HEALTH & SAFETY

A-
ATHLETICS

B
COMPUTERS

A
NIGHTLIFE

B+
FACILITIES

A-
GREEK LIFE

B-
CAMPUS DINING

C
DRUG SCENE

B+
OFF-CAMPUS DINING

B-
CAMPUS STRICTNESS

C+
CAMPUS HOUSING

B-
PARKING

B
OFF-CAMPUS HOUSING

A-
TRANSPORTATION

B
DIVERSITY

B
WEATHER

Overall Experience

Students Speak Out On...
Overall Experience

ℚ Awesome

I really love everything here- from the brick buildings to proximity of everything. I knew from the moment I stepped on the campus, this was where I belonged.

ℚ I Love FSU

I feel i made an amazing decision on where to attend college. I love FSU and i love tallahassee, i strongly reccomend this university to any incoming freshman.

Q I Love FSU

I love attending FSU. I love how beautiful the campus is and they're always trying to have something fun going on around campus. The people at the school are nice and friendly and it offers a quality education.

Q Its Fun Here

Very big school, lots to do, student government seems very cool. classes are fun, campus is very attractive.

Q Best Experience Ever

I love being at this school but if you aren't careful the social life can take over. I was lucky and joined a student organization called Alpha Kappa Psi, which has opened my horizons to new business opportunities. I have also met my best friends in this organizations. In the end this was my top choice i do not regret it!

Q FSU-Simply the Best

My experience at FSU has been simply wonderful! The student body is extremely friendly. The professors are very qualified and are very easy to approach, despite the large class sizes. There is plenty to do on campus. There are 3 dining halls, more than 10 other eating options, a state of the art gym, a massive library, a movie theater, and plenty of sporting events to enjoy, all right on campus. FSU will offer great opportunities and experiences to all.

Q Why I Love Florida State.

Florida State has a lot to offer its students if they work hard and take advantage. There are many many distractions here so staying focused is key...there will always be fun things to do and its pretty much the same so your not missing out on much that u cant part take in later. Faculty and fellow students are quite warming here, it is easy to meet people and get a sense that the faculty truly cares about you. The sense of unity becomes prominently apparent when a huge chunk of the student body attends football games.

Q The College Experience

I love Florida State University. You basically get it all. A great sports program, excellent academics, a terrific night life and it's absolutely beautiful in Tallahassee. We are located in the capital so there is a major advantage for political science majors. It seems like all of our programs are top ranked in the nation and I've never heard of someone not getting the most out of their time here.

The College Prowler Take On...
Overall Experience

You would be hard-pressed to find a graduate of Florida State University who doesn't have fond memories of the years they spent on campus. Current students will also agree that they are happy with their decision to attend school here. There is something for everyone, from athletics to academia, and you would have a hard time finding a more comfortable setting than Tallahassee. It has so much to offer, from exciting nightlife to beautiful weather.

Although it bears the reputation of a party school, FSU also has a growing reputation for turning out some of the best and brightest graduates in the entire nation. The school is now turning its focus on research, which should appeal to those interested in science and mathematics. But never fear, FSU also emphasizes the arts through their award-winning film and theater departments. From math and science, to the arts, FSU offers a vast array of eclectic degrees, which will be nothing but helpful later in your life. Choosing which college to attend is not an easy decision, but if you're looking for the perfect combination of a good education and a good time, you can't do much better than Florida State University.

The Inside Scoop

The Lowdown On...
The Inside Scoop

School Slang
The BLG: Broward, Landis, and Gilchrist residence halls
Club Stroz: Strozier Library
Fresh: Fresh Food Company
JRB: Jennie Murphree, Reynolds, and Bryan residence halls
The Rez: FSU Reservation
SLC: Student Life Cinema
The Swan: Suwannee Room
The Union: Oglesby Union

Things I Wish I Knew Before Coming To School
• Budgeting money.
• How important it is to meet with your advisor on a regular basis.
• How much you miss your family.

- How quickly it was going to pass.
- Just how humid North Florida can be.
- That it's expensive to eat out every night.

Tips to Succeed

- Don't rely on the notes written in used textbooks by the previous owners.
- Don't skip too many classes.
- Don't study on Landis Green in the summer. There are too many beautiful people.
- Get to know your instructors, and make sure they know who you are.
- If the professor offers a chance for extra credit, take it.

Traditions

Fountain Fling: Another demented tradition is skinny dipping in Westcott Fountain. To make it all the more interesting, the school now has a live Web-cam recording the fountain 24 hours a day.

Planting of the Spear: Possibly the most famous tradition at FSU is the planting of the spear by Chief Osceola, played by a lucky student. Prior to kickoff, Chief Osceola, riding his horse, Renegade, gallops onto the field and plants a flaming spear at midfield to begin every home game.

Sex at the Stadium: One tradition that has become increasingly difficult to pull off is having sex on the 50-yard line at Doak Campbell Stadium. Unfortunately, recent renovations have made it much more secure than it used to be, and the success rate has dropped off dramatically.

Sod Cemetery: The sod cemetery began when the first piece of sod was buried in the corner of the Florida State practice field, and a monument was placed to commemorate a road victory against Georgia in 1960. The tradition of planting a piece of sod from a road win stuck and is continued to this day.

Urban Legends

- It is said that the Pensacola Street Bridge was closed and torn down because head football coach Bobby Bowden didn't like the fact that people could stand on it and watch the football team practice inside Doak Campbell Stadium.

• Strozier Library is rumored to be haunted.

• The school is supposedly built on an ancient Seminole Indian burial ground. Hence the mascot.

Students Speak Out On...
The Inside Scoop

Q Unique
We have an amazing Business program, theater program, and education program. Research is being done alot at the school and we have huge programs as well as smaller ones.

Q Florida State University!!!
Florida State University is a pretty diverse school. Although I heard the opposite from others before I came here, I found that there are many different kinds of people with lots to offer. Making friends isn't hard with all the friendly students, and teachers are close with students and teach rather well. I knew I wanted to come to this school, and enjoy the city and college life. I hope to win this scholarship (and others) because they will help me out very much since I plan on staying in school for a while. I would like to get my PhD in Forensics Psychology, and am hoping to make it there successfully (if all financial issues don't prevent me from reaching there!) and comfortably. This school is great because there are many programs designed specifically for one's major, and the advisors are very helpful. Overall, it is casual and seems like an ideal-type school.

Q Seminole Pride
Just the overall feeling of being in a school with such great tradition is incredible! The architectural beauty of the campus is just breath taking and captivating and makes me proud of being a 'Nole. The weather is great and their Psychology department is amazing!

Q Small Size Feel

FSU is a huge university, but the campus is so compact that it doesn't feel that way.

Q FSU

Florida State University is unique in many ways. One of the most unique is that the University resides in the state's capitol. The campus is beautiful. Most buildings are made out of brick. Even the recently built buildings. It is a awesome location for a school!

Q Social Scene Is Great

There is always something to do and somewhere to go, as long as you like drinking.

Q Florida State

There are a lot of cool and unique things about this school. We are the only University to have our own circus, where the students organize it as well as perform. You can take classes to be a part of it. We also have the biggest intramural fields in the country, so we have nice facilities for everyone to play. Also, we have one of the largest and best Study Abroad Programs, which I hear are the most fun that people ever have.

Q Beautiful Campus With Excelent Academics

Florida State University has one of the most beautiful campuses I have ever seen. Even after a little more than a year, i still am amazed by the scenery walking to class. The school spirit is alive and well, especially during game days. Even with this the academics are extremely good. All of my Prof's really seem to enjoy what they are doing and really want the students to learn the material rather than just make the grade.

Jobs & Internships

The Lowdown On...
Jobs & Internships

Career Center
University Center, Building A, Suite 4100
(850) 644-6431
www.career.fsu.edu

Employment Services?
Yes

Placement Services?
Yes

Other Career Services
Career advising
Career development class
Career expositions
Career portfolios
Co-op/internships (paid and unpaid)
Job shadow program
Library with programs
that can help you
explore occupations, find
post-secondary and graduate
schools, obtain financial aid,

conduct self-assessments,
Mock interviews
On-campus interviews

Advice

Once you figure out what it is you want to do, begin exploring all the options available. Don't be afraid to ask questions, and be persistent when necessary. You won't get far if you expect a job to just fall in your lap. Be proactive.

Alumni & Post-Grads

The Lowdown On...
Alumni & Post-Grads

Alumni Office
Florida State University Alumni Association
1030 W. Tennessee St.
Phone: (850) 644-2761
alumni.fsu.edu

Major Alumni Events
Breakfast with Bobby Bowden
Canoe trips
Class reunions
Pre-game receptions

Services Available
Alumni travel programs
AVIS rental program
Career services
Discount at Office Max
Discount on moving services from Atlantic Relocation Systems
Group rates on auto and homeowners insurance with Liberty Mutual Insurance Group
Hertz rental program
Membership to FSU credit union

Networking in local and regional Seminole Club activities and programming Priority points assignment for athletic ticket purchases

Alumni Publications

Florida State Times magazine

Did You Know?

Famous FSU Alumni

Alan Ball (Attendee '80) – Academy Award-winning writer of American Beauty; creator of HBO's Six Feet Under

Tara Dawn Holland Christensen (Class of '94) – Miss America 1997

Rita Coolidge (Class of '67) – Two-time Grammy Award-winning vocalist

Lee Corso (Class of '58) – College football analyst for ESPN sports

Barbara Harris (Class of '78) – Editor of Shape magazine

Jim Morrison (Attendee '62) – Musician

Burt Reynolds (Attendee '58) – Award-winning actor and director

Deion Sanders (Class of '88) – Athlete

Richard Simmons (Class of '70) – Diet Guru

Norm Thagard (Class of '66) – Astronaut

Robert Urich (Class of '68) – Actor

Student Organizations

The Lowdown On...

ROTC
Air Force ROTC: Yes
Navy ROTC: Yes
Army ROTC: Yes

Student Activities Offered

Acabelles
Accounting Society
Activists for Gay Equality (AGE)
Amnesty International
Anthropological Society
APEX: Florida State Asian Greek Interest Group
Applied Sport Psychology (FSU-ASP)
Arab Cultural Association
Archon
Art History Association
Azucar Dance
Baha'i Unity Group
Ballroom Dance Club
Best Buddies
Beta Beta Beta Biological Honor Society
Bhakti Yoga Club
Catalyst
Chabad at FSU
Chi Alpha Christian Fellowship
Chinese American Student Association
Choral Association
Club Managers Association
Code Red
College Bowl
Collegiate Music Educators National Conference
Cuban-American Student Association
Cuong Nhu Martial Arts Club
Dance Student Advisory Council
Federalist Society

Fellowship of Christian Athletes
Fire and Hammer Collegiate Ministry
First Baptist Church College Ministry
First Collegiate Leaders Actively Saving Souls (1st CLASS)
Fishing Club, FSU
Garnet and Gold Key
Geography and Environmental Studies Student Association (GESSA)
Geriatric Interest Group
Get Carded
Global Talk
Golden Key International Honour Society
Gospel Choir, FSU
Green Party
Habitat for Humanity
Hablemos Español
Heritage House Student Fellowship
Hip Hop Club
Homeless Expression and Art (HEArt)
Honors Council, FSU
Independent Filmmaker's League
Indian Students Association
International Law Society
International Relations Organization
InterVarsity Christian Fellowship
Investment Firm, FSU
Japanese Animation Club of Tallahassee (J.A.C.T)

Jazz Society
Jeep Club
The Joining: Yoga Union, FSU
Journal of Land Use and
Environmental Law
Journal of Transnational
KARMA (Knowing About
Responsible Management of
Alcohol and other drugs)
Kiteboarding Association
Kollage Dance Troupe
Korean Undergraduate
Student Association (KUSA)
La Cosa Nostra
Ladies Misbehavior Society
Law and Policy
Les Meilleurs
If Association
Management Information
Systems
Marriage and Family Therapy
Graduate Student
Association
Medieval Studies Student
Association
Mock Trial Team, FSU
College of Law
Molecular Biophysics
Graduate Student
Organization
Mortar Board
Movimiento Estudiantil
Chicano de Aztlan (M.E.Ch.A)
Multicultural Association of
Pre-health Students (MAPS)
Multimedia Composers
Group
Music Theory Society
Musicians Student Union
NAACP

National Association of
Business Economics, FSU
Chapter
National Council of Negro
Women
National Science Teachers
Association
National Society for
Minorities in Hospitality
National Society of Black
Engineers
National Society of
Collegiate Scholars
Navigators, The
Ob/Gyn Interest Group
Objectivism, FSU
of America
Omicron Delta Kappa
Oncoming Traffic
Opera Students Association
Oscar Arias Sanchez Hispanic
Honor Society
Outlaw
Pagan Student Association
Paintball, FSU
PE Majors Club
Pediatric Interest Group
The People's Club
Phase 2
Phlava Dance Company
Pie Club, FSU
Political Science Graduate
Students Association
Pre-Physician Assistant Club
Pre-Veterinary Club
Professional Management
Association
Progressive Black Men, Inc.
Progressive Student
Assembly

Public Administration
Graduate Association
Public Debate Society
Public Interest Law Students
Association
Puerto Rican Student
Association
Racquet Sports Club
Ranger Challenge
Real Estate Society
Reflections Modeling Troupe
Reformed University
Fellowship
Russian Club, FSU
Sailing Association
Seminole Dance Force
Seminole Scuba Club
Semper Fidelis Society
Shotokan Karate Club
SISTUHS, Inc.
Social Work Doctoral Student
Organization
Society for Early Music
Society for Musicology
Society for Performance
Management
Society for Poetic Elements
Society for Women's
Advancement in Philosophy
Society of Automotive
Engineers (SAE)
Society of Composers
Society of Environmental
Engineers
Society of Physics Students
Society of Women Engineers
The Source
Spanish American Law
Students Association (SALSA)
SPEAK (Service Promoting

Educational Argumentation
Knowledge)
Sports Medicine Interest
Group
Sports Official Association
STRIKE
Student Archaeology Club
Student Bar Association
Student Dietetics Association
Student Economic
Association
Student Interest Group in
Neurology (SIGN)
Students for Genital Integrity
Students for the Ethical
Treatment of Animals (SETA)
Students for Understanding
Nutrition Now (SUNN)
Students in Free Enterprise
Students United for Peace
and Justice
Suburban Rebellion Wrestling
Swing Dance Union, FSU
Synchronizied Swimming
Club
Synoptikos
Tallahassee Bar Association
Tallahassee Campus
Ministries
Tallahassee Chess Club
Tallahassee College Outreach
Tallahassee Triple Threat
Alliance
Tau Beta Sigma
Teach for America
Thalassic Society
Tolerance and Dialogue
Group
Total Health Empowerment
for Ladies of Color

Trailblazers, FSU
Tuesday Night Fellowship
Turkish Student Association
UMADD
Undergraduate Art History
Association
Union of Freethinking
Students
United Christian Artists
Unity Party
University Flying Club
University Orchestras
University Unitarian
Universalists
Unveiled, The Collegiate
Ministry of Northwoods
Victory Campus Ministries
Vision
VOX: Voices for Planned
Parenthood
W.E.B. Dubois Honor Society
Wealth Builders
Wesley Foundation
When Illnesses Strike Due to
Our Miseducation (WISDOM)
Wilderness Medicine Society
Women in Computer Science
Women's FSUltimate
Women's Law Symposium
World Music Society
Wushu

The Best

The **BEST** Things

1. FSU Seminole football

2. Warm weather

3. FSU Flying High Circus

4. Checking out the "student bodies" on Landis Green

5. FSU Reservation at Lake Bradford

6. Faculty that cares about the students

7. Free movies at the SLB

8. State-of-the-art computer labs

9. Quality academics

10. The parties, both on and off campus

The Worst

The **WORST** Things

1. Student parking

2. The humidity in August

3. Airfare in and out of Tallahassee

4. The terrible roads in and around campus

5. Musty buildings

6. Anyplace that isn't air conditioned

7. Uncaring teaching assistants

8. More emphasis on athletics than academics

9. Outdated elevators

10. Dining hall food

Visiting

The Lowdown On...
Visiting

Campus Tours
Campus tours run most Mondays through Fridays (except on holidays, between semesters, during finals spring break). They last about 90 minutes and are conducted by a student ambassador. Check out visit.fsu.edu for more information

Virtual Tour of Campus
www.fsutour.org

Interviews & Information Sessions
Contact the FSU Office of Admissions at (850) 644-3246 or schedule your visit online by going tovisit.fsu.edu .

Words to Know

Academic Probation – A suspension imposed on a student if he or she fails to keep up with the school's minimum academic requirements. Those unable to improve their grades after receiving this warning can face dismissal.

Beer Pong/Beirut – A drinking game involving cups of beer arranged in a pyramid shape on each side of a table. The goal is to get a ping pong ball into one of the opponent's cups by throwing the ball or hitting it with a paddle. If the ball lands in a cup, the opponent is required to drink the beer.

Bid – An invitation from a fraternity or sorority to 'pledge' (join) that specific house.

Blue-Light Phone – Brightly-colored phone posts with a blue light bulb on top. These phones exist for security purposes and are located at various outside locations around most campuses. In an emergency, a student can pick up one of these phones (free of charge) to connect with campus police or a security escort.

Campus Police – Police who are specifically assigned to a given institution. Campus police are typically not regular city officers; they are employed by the university in a full-time capacity.

Club Sports – A level of sports that falls somewhere between varsity and intramural. If a student is unable to commit to a varsity team but has a lot of passion for athletics, a club sport could be a better, less intense option. Even less demanding, intramural (IM) sports often involve no traveling and considerably less time.

Cocaine – An illegal drug. Also known as "coke" or "blow," cocaine often resembles a white crystalline or powdery substance. It is highly addictive and dangerous.

Common Application – An application with which students can apply to multiple schools.

Course Registration – The period of official class selection for the upcoming quarter or semester. Prior to registration, it is best to prepare several back-up courses in case a particular class becomes full. If a course is full, students can place themselves on the waitlist, although this still does not guarantee entry.

Division Athletics – Athletic classifications range from Division I to Division III. Division IA is the most competitive, while Division III is considered to be the least competitive.

Dorm – A dorm (or dormitory) is an on-campus housing facility. Dorms can provide a range of options from suite-style rooms to more communal options that include shared bathrooms. Most first-year students live in dorms. Some upperclassmen who wish to stay on campus also choose this option.

Early Action – An application option with which a student can apply to a school and receive an early acceptance response without a binding commitment. This system is becoming less and less available.

Early Decision – An application option that students should use only if they are certain they plan to attend the school in question. If a student applies using the early decision option and is admitted, he or she is required and bound to attend that university. Admission rates are usually higher among students who apply through early decision, as the student is clearly indicating that the school is his or her first choice.

Ecstasy – An illegal drug. Also known as "E" or "X," ecstasy looks like a pill and most resembles an aspirin. Considered a party drug, ecstasy is very dangerous and can be deadly.

Ethernet – An extremely fast Internet connection available in most university-owned residence halls. To use an Ethernet connection properly, a student will need a network card and cable for his or her computer.

Fake ID – A counterfeit identification card that contains false information. Most commonly, students get fake IDs with altered birthdates so that they appear to be older than 21 (and therefore of legal drinking age). Even though it is illegal, many college students have fake IDs in hopes of purchasing alcohol or getting into bars.

Frosh – Slang for "freshman" or "freshmen."

Hazing – Initiation rituals administered by some fraternities or sororities as part of the pledging process. Many universities have outlawed hazing due to its degrading, and sometimes dangerous, nature.

Intramurals (IMs) – A popular, and usually free, sport league in which students create teams and compete against one another. These sports vary in competitiveness and can include a range of activities—everything from billiards to water polo. IM sports are a great way to meet people with similar interests.

Keg – Officially called a half-barrel, a keg contains roughly 200 12-ounce servings of beer.

LSD – An illegal drug, also known as acid, this hallucinogenic drug most commonly resembles a tab of paper.

Marijuana – An illegal drug, also known as weed or pot; along with alcohol, marijuana is one of the most commonly found drugs on campuses across the country.

Major –The focal point of a student's college studies; a specific topic that is studied for a degree. Examples of majors include physics, English, history, computer science, economics, business, and music. Many students decide on a specific major before arriving on campus, while others are simply "undecided" until declaring a major. Those who are extremely interested in two areas can also choose to double major.

Meal Block – The equivalent of one meal. Students on a meal plan usually receive a fixed number of meals per week. Each meal, or "block," can be redeemed at the school's dining facilities in place of cash. Often, a student's weekly allotment of meal blocks will be forfeited if not used.

Minor – An additional focal point in a student's education. Often serving as a complement or addition to a student's main area of focus, a minor has fewer requirements and prerequisites to fulfill than a major. Minors are not required for graduation from most schools; however some students who want to explore many different interests choose to pursue both a major and a minor.

Mushrooms – An illegal drug. Also known as "'shrooms," this drug resembles regular mushrooms but is extremely hallucinogenic.

Off-Campus Housing – Housing from a particular landlord or rental group that is not affiliated with the university. Depending on the college, off-campus housing can range from extremely popular to non-existent. Students who choose to live off campus are typically given more freedom, but they also have to deal with possible subletting scenarios, furniture, bills, and other issues. In addition to these factors, rental prices and distance often affect a student's decision to move off campus.

Office Hours – Time that teachers set aside for students who have questions about coursework. Office hours are a good forum for students to go over any problems and to show interest in the subject material.

Pledging – The early phase of joining a fraternity or sorority, pledging takes place after a student has gone through rush and received a bid. Pledging usually lasts between one and two semesters. Once the pledging period is complete and a particular student has done everything that is required to become a member, that student is considered a brother or sister. If a fraternity or a sorority would decide to "haze" a group of students, this initiation would take place during the pledging period.

Private Institution – A school that does not use tax revenue to subsidize education costs. Private schools typically cost more than public schools and are usually smaller.

Prof – Slang for "professor."

Public Institution – A school that uses tax revenue to subsidize education costs. Public schools are often a good value for in-state residents and tend to be larger than most private colleges.

Quarter System (or Trimester System) – A type of academic calendar system. In this setup, students take classes for three academic periods. The first quarter usually starts in late September or early October and concludes right before Christmas. The second quarter usually starts around early to mid–January and finishes up around March or April. The last academic quarter, or "third quarter," usually starts in late March or early April and finishes up in late May or Mid-June. The fourth quarter is summer. The major difference between the quarter system and semester system is that students take more, less comprehensive courses under the quarter calendar.

RA (Resident Assistant) – A student leader who is assigned to a particular floor in a dormitory in order to help to the other students who live there. An RA's duties include ensuring student safety and providing assistance wherever possible.

Recitation – An extension of a specific course; a review session. Some classes, particularly large lectures, are supplemented with mandatory recitation sessions that provide a relatively personal class setting.

Rolling Admissions – A form of admissions. Most commonly found at public institutions, schools with this type of policy continue to accept students throughout the year until their class sizes are met. For example, some schools begin accepting students as early as December and will continue to do so until April or May.

Room and Board – This figure is typically the combined cost of a university-owned room and a meal plan.

Room Draw/Housing Lottery – A common way to pick on-campus room assignments for the following year. If a student decides to remain in university-owned housing, he or she is assigned a unique number that, along with seniority, is used to determine his or her housing for the next year.

Rush – The period in which students can meet the brothers and sisters of a particular chapter and find out if a given fraternity or sorority is right for them. Rushing a fraternity or a sorority is not a requirement at any school. The goal of rush is to give students who are serious about pledging a feel for what to expect.

Semester System – The most common type of academic calendar system at college campuses. This setup typically includes two semesters in a given school year. The fall semester starts around the end of August or early September and concludes before winter vacation. The spring semester usually starts in mid-January and ends in late April or May.

Student Center/Rec Center/Student Union – A common area on campus that often contains study areas, recreation facilities, and eateries. This building is often a good place to meet up with fellow students; depending on the school, the student center can have a huge role or a non-existent role in campus life.

Student ID – A university-issued photo ID that serves as a student's key to school-related functions. Some schools require students to show these cards in order to get into dorms, libraries, cafeterias, and other facilities. In addition to storing meal plan information, in some cases, a student ID can actually work as a debit card and allow students to purchase things from bookstores or local shops.

Suite – A type of dorm room. Unlike dorms that feature communal bathrooms shared by the entire floor, suites offer bathrooms shared only among the suite. Suite-style dorm rooms can house anywhere from two to ten students.

TA (Teacher's Assistant) – An undergraduate or grad student who helps in some manner with a specific course. In some cases, a TA will teach a class, assist a professor, grade assignments, or conduct office hours.

Undergraduate – A student in the process of studying for his or her bachelor's degree.

About the Author

Name: Cheryl Justis

Hometown: Daytona Beach, Fla.

Major:

Fun Fact:

Previous Contributors: Richard Bist

Pros and Cons

Still can't figure out if this is the right school for you?
You've already read through this in-depth guide;
why not list the pros and cons? It will really help
with narrowing down your decision and determining
whether or not this school is right for you.

Pros	Cons
....	....
....	....
....	....
....	....
....	....
....	....
....	....
....	....
....	....
....	....
....	....
....	....

Pros and Cons

Still can't figure out if this is the right school for you?
You've already read through this in-depth guide;
why not list the pros and cons? It will really help
with narrowing down your decision and determining
whether or not this school is right for you.

Pros	Cons
....	....
....	....
....	....
....	....
....	....
....	....
....	....
....	....
....	....
....	....
....	....
....	....

Notes

Notes

....

....

....

....

....

....

....

....

....

....

....

....

....

....

....

Notes

....
....
....
....
....
....
....
....
....
....
....
....
....
....
....

Notes

Notes

....

....

....

....

....

....

....

....

....

....

....

....

....

....

....

Notes

....

....

....

....

....

....

....

....

....

....

....

....

....

....

....

Notes

....

....

....

....

....

....

....

....

....

....

....

....

....

....

....

Notes

....

....

....

....

....

....

....

....

....

....

....

....

....

....

Notes

....
....
....
....
....
....
....
....
....
....
....
....
....
....
....

Notes

....
....
....
....
....
....
....
....
....
....
....
....
....
....
....

Notes

....

....

....

....

....

....

....

....

....

....

....

....

....

....

....

Notes

....

....

....

....

....

....

....

....

....

....

....

....

....

....

....

Notes

....

....

....

....

....

....

....

....

....

....

....

....

....

....

....

Review Your School!

Let your voice be heard.

Every year, thousands of students take our online survey to share their opinions about campus life.

Now's your chance to help millions of high school students choose the right college for them.

Tell us what life is really like at your school by taking our online survey or even uploading your own photos and videos!

And as our thanks to you for participating in our survey, we'll enter you into a random drawing for our $1,000 Monthly Survey Scholarship!

For more information, check out
www.collegeprowler.com/survey

Write For Us!

Express your opinion. Get published!

Interested in being a published author? College Prowler is always on the lookout for current college students across the country to write the guides for their schools.

The contributing author position is a unique opportunity for eager college students to bolster their résumés and portfolios, become published authors both online and in print, and gain tremendous exposure to millions of high school students nationwide.

For more details, visit
www.collegeprowler.com/careers

Albion College
Alfred University
Allegheny College
Alverno College
American Intercontinental
   University Online
American University
Amherst College
Arizona State University
Ashford University
The Art Institute of
   California – Orange
   County
Auburn University
Austin College
Babson College
Ball State University
Bard College
Barnard College
Barry University
Baruch College
Bates College
Bay Path College
Baylor University
Beloit College
Bentley University
Berea College
Binghamton University
Birmingham Southern
   College
Bob Jones University
Boston College
Boston University
Bowdoin College
Bradley University
Brandeis University
Brigham Young University
Brigham Young
   University – Idaho
Brown University
Bryant University
Bryn Mawr College
Bucknell University
Cal Poly Pomona
California College
   of the Arts
California Institute
   of Technology
California Polytechnic
   State University
California State University
   – Monterey Bay
California State University
   – Northridge
California State University
   – San Marcos
Carleton College
Carnegie Mellon University
Case Western Reserve
   University
Catawba College
Catholic University
   of America

Centenary College
   of Louisiana
Centre College
Chapman University
Chatham University
City College of New York
City College of
   San Francisco
Claflin University
Claremont McKenna
   College
Clark Atlanta University
Clark University
Clemson University
Cleveland State University
Colby College
Colgate University
College of Charleston
College of Mount
   Saint Vincent
College of Notre
   Dame of Maryland
College of the Holy Cross
College of William & Mary
College of Wooster
Colorado College
Columbia College Chicago
Columbia University
Concordia University
   – Wisconsin
Connecticut College
Contra Costa College
Cornell College
Cornell University
Creighton University
CUNY Lehman College
CUNY Queens College
CUNY Queensborough
   Community College
Dalton State College
Dartmouth College
Davidson College
De Anza College
Del Mar College
Denison University
DePaul University
DePauw University
Diablo Valley College
Dickinson College
Dordt College
Drexel University
Duke University
Duquesne University
Earlham College
East Carolina University
Eckerd College
El Paso Community
   College
Elon University
Emerson College
Emory University
Fashion Institute of Design
   & Merchandising

Fashion Institute of
   Technology
Ferris State University
Florida Atlantic University
Florida Southern College
Florida State University
Fordham University
Franklin & Marshall
   College
Franklin Pierce University
Frederick Community
   College
Freed-Hardeman
   University
Furman University
Gannon University
Geneva College
George Mason University
George Washington
   University
Georgetown University
Georgia Institute of
   Technology
Georgia Perimeter College
Georgia State University
Germanna Community
   College
Gettysburg College
Gonzaga University
Goucher College
Grinnell College
Grove City College
Guilford College
Gustavus Adolphus
   College
Hamilton College
Hampshire College
Hampton University
Hanover College
Harvard University
Harvey Mudd College
Hastings College
Haverford College
Hillsborough Community
   College
Hofstra University
Hollins University
Howard University
Hunter College (CUNY)
Idaho State University
Illinois State University
Illinois Wesleyan University
Indiana Univ.–Purdue Univ.
   Indianapolis (IUPUI)
Indiana University
Iowa State University
Ithaca College
Jackson State University
James Madison University
Johns Hopkins University
Juniata College
Kansas State University
Kaplan University

Kent State University
Kenyon College
La Roche College
Lafayette College
Lawrence University
Lehigh University
Lewis & Clark College
Linfield College
Los Angeles City College
Los Angeles Valley College
Louisiana College
Louisiana State University
Loyola College in
   Maryland
Loyola Marymount
   University
Loyola University Chicago
Luther College
Macalester College
Macomb Community
   College
Manhattan College
Manhattanville College
Marlboro College
Marquette University
Maryville University
Massachusetts College
   of Art & Design
Massachusetts Institute
   of Technology
McGill University
Merced College
Mercyhurst College
Messiah College
Miami University
Michigan State University
Middle Tennessee
   State University
Middlebury College
Millsaps College
Minnesota State
   University – Moorhead
Missouri State University
Montana State University
Montclair State University
Moorpark College
Mount Holyoke College
Muhlenberg College
New College of Florida
New York University
North Carolina A&T
   State University
North Carolina State
   University
Northeastern University
Northern Arizona
   University
Northern Illinois University
Northwest Florida
   State College
Northwestern College
   – Saint Paul
Northwestern University

Oakwood University
Oberlin College
Occidental College
Oglethorpe University
Ohio State University
Ohio University
Ohio Wesleyan University
Old Dominion University
Onondaga Community College
Oral Roberts University
Pace University
Palm Beach State College
Penn State Altoona
Penn State Brandywine
Penn State University
Pepperdine University
Pitzer College
Pomona College
Princeton University
Providence College
Purdue University
Radford University
Ramapo College of New Jersey
Reed College
Rensselaer Polytechnic Institute
Rhode Island School of Design
Rhodes College
Rice University
Rider University
Robert Morris University
Rochester Institute of Technology
Rocky Mountain College of Art & Design
Rollins College
Rowan University
Rutgers University
Sacramento State
Saint Francis University
Saint Joseph's University
Saint Leo University
Salem College
Salisbury University
Sam Houston State University
Samford University
San Diego State University
San Francisco State University
Santa Clara University
Santa Fe College
Sarah Lawrence College
Scripps College
Seattle University
Seton Hall University
Simmons College
Skidmore College
Slippery Rock University
Smith College

South Texas College
Southern Methodist University
Southwestern University
Spelman College
St. John's College – Annapolis
St. John's University
St. Louis University
St. Mary's University
St. Olaf College
Stanford University
State University of New York – Purchase College
State University of New York at Fredonia
State University of New York at Oswego
Stetson University
Stevens-Henager College
Stony Brook University (SUNY)
Susquehanna University
Swarthmore College
Syracuse University
Taylor University
Temple University
Tennessee State University
Texas A&M University
Texas Christian University
Texas Tech
The Community College of Baltimore County
Towson University
Trinity College (Conn.)
Trinity University (Texas)
Troy University
Truman State University
Tufts University
Tulane University
Union College
University at Albany (SUNY)
University at Buffalo (SUNY)
University of Alabama
University of Arizona
University of Arkansas
University of Arkansas at Little Rock
University of California – Berkeley
University of California – Davis
University of California – Irvine
University of California – Los Angeles
University of California – Merced
University of California – Riverside
University of California – San Diego

University of California – Santa Barbara
University of California – Santa Cruz
University of Central Florida
University of Chicago
University of Cincinnati
University of Colorado
University of Connecticut
University of Delaware
University of Denver
University of Florida
University of Georgia
University of Hartford
University of Illinois
University of Illinois at Chicago
University of Iowa
University of Kansas
University of Kentucky
University of Louisville
University of Maine
University of Maryland
University of Maryland – Baltimore County
University of Massachusetts
University of Miami
University of Michigan
University of Minnesota
University of Mississippi
University of Missouri
University of Montana
University of Mount Union
University of Nebraska
University of Nevada – Las Vegas
University of New Hampshire
University of North Carolina
University of North Carolina – Greensboro
University of Notre Dame
University of Oklahoma
University of Oregon
University of Pennsylvania
University of Phoenix
University of Pittsburgh
University of Puget Sound
University of Rhode Island
University of Richmond
University of Rochester
University of San Diego
University of San Francisco
University of South Carolina
University of South Dakota
University of South Florida
University of Southern California
University of St Thomas – Texas

University of Tampa
University of Tennessee
University of Tennessee at Chattanooga
University of Texas
University of Utah
University of Vermont
University of Virginia
University of Washington
University of Western Ontario
University of Wisconsin
University of Wisconsin – Stout
Urbana University
Ursinus College
Valencia Community College
Valparaiso University
Vanderbilt University
Vassar College
Villanova University
Virginia Commonwealth University
Virginia Tech
Virginia Union University
Wagner College
Wake Forest University
Warren Wilson College
Washington & Jefferson College
Washington & Lee University
Washington University in St. Louis
Wellesley College
Wesleyan University
West Los Angeles College
West Point Military Academy
West Virginia University
Western Illinois University
Western Kentucky University
Wheaton College (Ill.)
Wheaton College (Mass.)
Whitman College
Wilkes University
Willamette University
Williams College
Xavier University
Yale University
Youngstown State University